Hand Weaving

An Introduction to Weaving on 2, 3 and 4 Harnesses

Hand Weaving

An Introduction to Weaving on 2, 3 and 4 Harnesses

Mad Duchemin

VNR VAN NOSTRAND REINHOLD COMPANY
NEW YORK CINCINNATI TORONTO LONDON MELBOURNE

©Dessain et Tolra, Paris
Originally published in France as
'Le Tissage à la Main Sur 2, 3, et 4 Lames'

English edition first published 1975

Printed in Great Britain

Published in 1975 by
Van Nostrand Reinhold Company
A Division of Litton Educational
Publishing, Inc.
450 West 33rd Street
New York, NY 10001, USA.
16 15 14 13 12 11 10 9 8 7 6 5 4 3 2 1

**Library of Congress Cataloging in
Publication Data**

Duchemin, Mad.
  Hand weaving.

  Translation of Le tissage à la main sur
4 lames.
  1. Hand weaving. I. Title.
TT848.D7613   746.1'4   75-7142
ISBN 0-442-22183-5

Contents

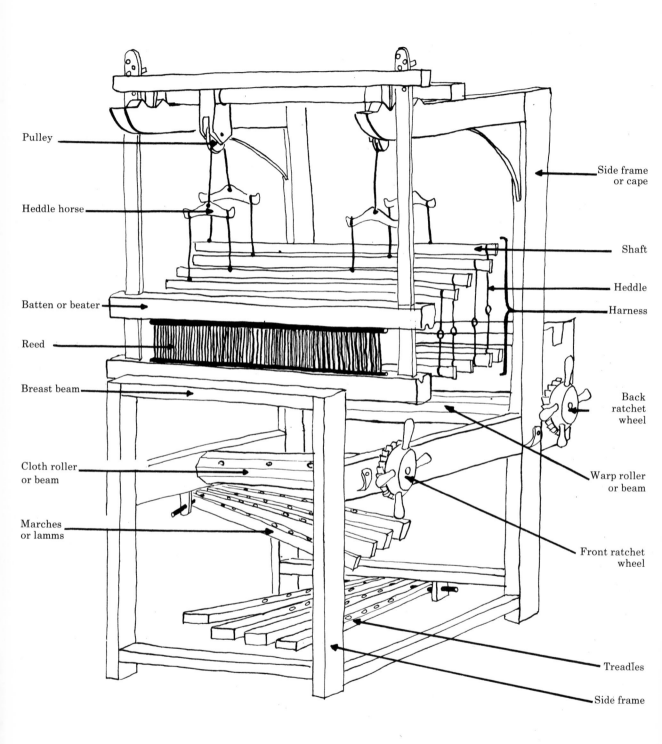

Pulley

Heddle horse

Batten or beater

Reed

Breast beam

Cloth roller
or beam

Marches
or lamms

Side frame
or cape

Shaft

Heddle

Harness

Back
ratchet
wheel

Warp roller
or beam

Front ratchet
wheel

Treadles

Side frame

Introduction

Weaving is a very old technique, its origins can be traced back to the enclosures of interlaced branches made by early man.

At first no more than a simple frame, the loom has undergone continuous development throughout the ages, prompted by the needs of generations of weavers who needed a tool which would enable them to work more quickly at their repetitive task.

Weaving is the process of interlacing the warp threads, wound onto the back roller and stretched evenly through the loom, with the weft threads, wound onto a shuttle and thrown from one selvedge to the other, passing above some warp threads and below others. This interlacing creates the woven fabric.

This book is written primarily for beginners, and thus it is first necessary to describe the various parts of a loom and its mechanism. Then follows a step-by-step description in logical sequence of the different processes involved in making a warp and in preparing and setting up a loom. This leads to a simple discussion of cloth structure and the basic weaves.

In 'Beginning the weaving', the emphasis is placed on two essentials, the action of weaving, which is the principal ingredient of success, and mistakes, which can always be remedied.

The second section presents a number of possibilities for weaving on two, three or four shafts. By no means exhaustive, it suggests just a few ideas from the vast range of woven textiles.

Operation of the loom and the technique of weaving

1 The loom

There are two main types of loom, the hand (or table) loom with levers, and the foot-power loom with treadles.

The table looms are usually rising shed. The shafts work independently, and when one is raised for the passage of the shuttle, it lifts all the warp threads that are drawn through the eyes of its heddles. The other threads do not move.

Foot-power looms are simply a framework to support the three essentials

(a) a back roller from which the warp is wound
(b) a front roller onto which the finished cloth is wound
(c) a harness in the centre which divides the warp threads for weaving

1.1 The front and back rollers

These rollers are provided with a mechanism which prevents them from turning and so maintains a tension on the warp. The sheet of warp threads is stretched evenly, and runs horizontally across the loom from back to front, coming up from the warp roller, over the back beam, forward to the breast beam and then downwards and inwards to the cloth roller.

Two cross sticks are inserted in the warp between the back beam and the harness, with the even threads above a stick and the odd threads below or vice versa, to prevent the threads from becoming tangled.

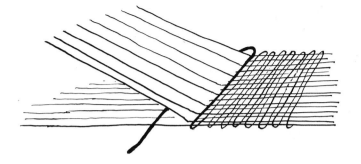

Movement of the warp with a
rising shed

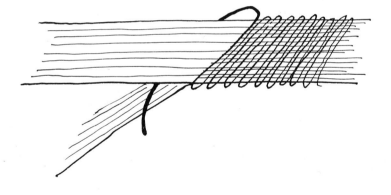

Movement of the warp with a
sinking shed

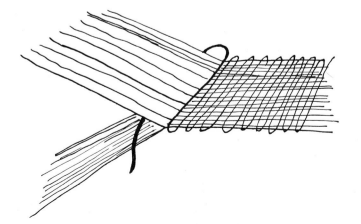

Movement of the warp with a
rising and sinking shed

11

1.2 The harness

This is the most important part of the loom. It divides the warp threads into two layers so that the weft threads can be passed under or over the correct warp threads with a shuttle. In the simplest harness, for plain weave, the even threads rise and the odd threads sink, (or vice versa), to form an opening or shed for the passage of the shuttle. The threads of the warp pass through the heddles, which are small loops of cotton or linen twine, with an eye, or a 'mail' of metal or glass, in the middle. The heddles are carried on two parallel sticks across the loom. Heddles (or heals) are also made of wire. A set of heddles on their sticks is called a shaft and a set of two or more shafts working together is called a harness. A loom can have a harness of from two to sixteen shafts, which is the practical limit. Beyond that a dobby loom or a Jacquard loom would be used.

The shafts are moved by a system of levers, which, at first sight, may seem to be a little complicated.

The shed is the opening between the two layers of threads

A string heddle

opposite
The back and front rollers and the harness of a foot-power loom

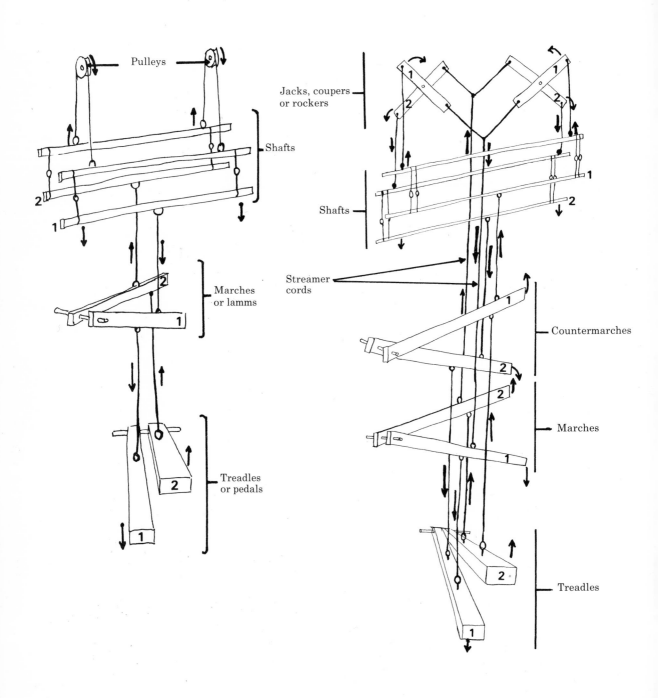

Pulleys

Jacks, coupers
or rockers

Shafts

Shafts

Marches
or lamms

Streamer
cords

Countermarches

Treadles
or pedals

Marches

Treadles

Movement of the shafts on a
counterbalanced loom

Movement of the shafts on a
countermarch loom

1.3　The movement of the shafts on a rising and sinking shed loom

There are two alternative ways of operating the shafts, the counterbalanced and the countermarch systems.

Counterbalanced system
In a two-shaft harness with pulleys for a plain weave cloth, the two shafts, numbered 1 and 2 from front to back, are tied by cords of equal length to two lamms, also numbered 1 and 2 in the same order, each shaft being tied to its own lamm. Each lamm is then tied to one of the treadles, again using cords of equal length. When one of the treadles is depressed it pulls down the lamm to which it is tied and so brings down the shaft tied to that particular lamm. The cord which goes up from this shaft over the pulley comes down with the shaft and so raises the shaft on the other end.

Countermarch system
With countermarches a better and more even shed is obtained, as the rising shed no longer depends on the sinking shafts to produce it. This system is always used on looms wider than 1 m (40 in.). Each shaft is hung from the outer ends of a pair of pivoted jacks or rockers, which are in turn tied by their inner ends to a long streamer cord going down to the marches. The diagram shows the effect of operating the left treadle or pedal.

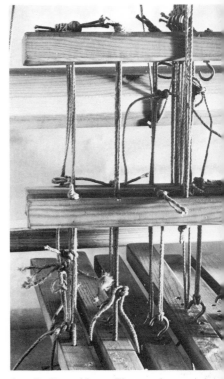

A well-adjusted loom. The marches and countermarches are horizontal

The downward movement of the treadle causes both march 1 and countermarch 2 to sink, as both of them are tied to the treadle being pressed down. The march pulls down the inner ends of number 1 jacks, which tilt, so that the outer ends rise and lift shaft 1 which is tied to them. The countermarch 2 pulls down shaft 2 which is tied directly to it.

The positive movement of the shaft in both directions allows a much more precise adjustment of the shed to give a clear passage to the shuttle.

1.4　The principles of adjustment for counterbalanced and countermarch looms

The sheet of warp threads must be flat, and must be level with the centre of the eyes of the heddles. This determines the height of the shafts and consequently the lengths of the cords from the shafts upwards to the pulleys or the jacks. All the levers, the marches, countermarches and the jacks, must be horizontal in the resting position. The height of the treadles varies according to the depth of the shed required. On a countermarch loom, the long cords are those which tie the treadles to the countermarches, and the short cords go from the treadles to the marches. The treadling draft gives the order in which the treadles are to be used, each change corresponding to a further shot of weft.

1.5 The shuttle

The weft is wound on a bobbin or a pirn of paper, cardboard, wood or metal and placed in a shuttle.

The design of the shuttle is independent of the design of the loom. It is usually made of wood, long and pointed at both ends, with a hollow in the centre to receive the bobbin or the pirn, and an eye in the side through which the weft unwinds.

Some accessories
1 ⎫
2 ⎬ Roller shuttles
3 Pirn shuttle or flying shuttle
4 Paddle
5 Bobbin winder
6 Bobbin for a roller shuttle
7 Bobbin
8 Paper quill for a bobbin for a roller shuttle
9 Reed hook

opposite
The warp threads form a single layer passing through the centres of the eyes of the heddles

There are many types of shuttle, but they can all be placed in two broad categories, according to the way that the weft unwinds

(a) shuttles in which the weft unwinds over the end of a pirn, which is held firmly on a central pin and does not turn. The eye for the weft is at one end of the bobbin cavity

(b) shuttles in which the weft unwinds from the side of a bobbin which is held loosely on a pin and revolves while unwinding. The eye for the weft is in the centre of the shuttle

Bobbin shuttles are used exclusively for throwing by hand, and heavy pirn shuttles are used in fly-shuttle weaving. There are also hand-thrown pirn shuttles, heavier than ordinary roller shuttles, which, owing to their greater weight, are easier to throw through the shed as they are not slowed down by friction as are the lighter shuttles.

1.6   The beater or batten

The beater usually hangs from the top of the loom, but in some types of loom it is pivoted at the bottom. It carries the reed, with which the weft is beaten-up by swinging the batten forwards against the cloth already woven. The bottom part is a thick block of wood, the race block, which carries the shuttle race. The weight of this block, combined with the speed acquired in weaving, ensures a good beat-up of the weft. There is a considerable strain on the beater

Loom with an underslung batten

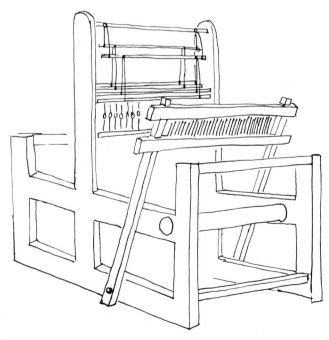

when weaving with a large number of warp threads, so it has to be rigidly constructed to prevent its twisting and causing faults in the cloth.

The simple batten is used for the hand-thrown shuttle whilst the fly-shuttle batten is used for throwing the shuttle mechanically. There is a box at each end of the shuttle-race, and the shuttle is sent backwards and forwards between the boxes by pulling on the picking cord hanging from the centre of the top of the batten.

1.7 The reed or sley

The shuttle lays a thread, a 'pick' of weft, as long as the warp is wide between the selvedges. The batten carries the reed, which beats-up the new weft against the previous threads, and sets it straight and to the correct length.

The reed consists of a series of vertical flat wires of steel or brass, set between the top and bottom 'baulks' or rods. The warp threads or 'ends' pass between the wires. Different reeds are used according to the density or 'sett' required. The sett and the length of the reed are usually indicated on the ends of continental reeds, the sett only on non-metric English reeds. The continental sett is stated as the number of threads to ten centimetres, so the numbers 20/10/90 would indicate that there were 20 dents per 10 cm in a 90 cm reed. The English Imperial reeds carry the number of dents to the inch. In both cases the numbers are stamped on the end wire of the reed. (See appendix for English–metric conversions.)

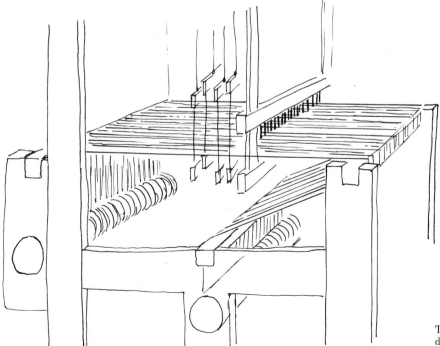

The warp threaded through the dents of the reed

1.8 The tenterhook

The width of the cloth as set in the reed can be maintained more easily in a heavy fabric by using a tenterhook or temple. The tenterhook is a flat strip of wood, made in two parts, which can be adjusted to the width of the warp in the reed. The bevelled ends of the tenterhook each carry a set of fine steel needles pointing downwards and outwards. The fabric can become narrower during weaving, due to too great a tension on the weft, so the tenterhook is set to the width, and the pins put through the cloth just inside the selvedge threads. The centre is pressed down and the locking ring slid into place. Every time that the warp is wound on, the tenterhook has to be moved up.

Two essential aspects emerge from this description of the loom

(a) the interlacing of the threads depends on the raising and lowering of the warp threads by the shafts
(b) the progress of the warp through the loom seems much more complex than that of the weft, which merely unwinds from a shuttle as it passes through the shed

Once a warp has been made and mounted on the loom, it is a fixed element in the cloth, whereas the weft is unlimited in its variety.

To prepare a loom for weaving and mount the warp is both long and exacting.

The tenterhook open and fixed in the selvedges

The tenterhook closed

2 Mounting the warp

The threads, at first handled separately whilst making the bobbins for warping, are brought together on the warping mill to form the complete warp or 'chain'. The chain is 'beamed', (wound onto the warp beam of the loom), then each thread is drawn through the eye of one of the heddles of the harness and through a dent in the reed. The warp is finally tied to the front stick, which in turn is attached to the cloth roller at the front of the loom. It remains only to tie up the treadles according to the weave plan being used and wind the bobbins before starting to weave.

2.1 The choice of warp

There is no definite rule in the choice of a warp. In the weaving industry precision instruments are used to check the threads, the regularity, the twist ratio, and the elastic recovery.

In hand weaving the warp thread must at least be strong enough to resist the tension which can be applied with the hands and then break with a snap. If it offers no resistance or breaks too easily it is of no use for a warp. Fibres of different types can be mixed in the same warp: linen, cotton, wool. The difference in the elasticity of the fibres can make the weaving onerous, but not impossible. Therein lies much of the richness and character of hand weaving. The warp represents the concept of a woven fabric; it is its foundation and has its dimensions.

The width, calculating the number of threads to the centimetre (inch)

The number of threads in the warp is determined by the width in centimetres (inches) and the number of threads to the centimetre (inch) or 'sett'. The width is multiplied by the sett, and this gives the total number of threads in the warp. For example, if a fabric 100 cm (36 in.) wide is to be woven with a warp which sets at 4 threads/cm, (10 ends/in.), then

> 100 (cm) × 4 (thds/cm) = 400 threads in the warp.
> 36 (in.) × 10 (ends/in.) = 360 threads in the warp.

To determine the number of threads to the centimetre (inch), the simplest way is to wind the threads round a ruler with the threads just touching without being cramped and count the number of threads to the centimetre (inch). About half this number is a good sett for a plain weave, slightly more than half for twills or hopsack weaves. A fine silk may have 16 threads/cm (40 ends/in.), mohair 2.5 or 3 (6 or 8), but there is nothing compulsory about this. It all depends on the appearance of the cloth and what is required of it. Although woven on the same warp of fine wool with a weft of cotton bouclé, there is an easily visible difference between the two samples which are illustrated. One is set at 7 (18) single threads/cm (in.), the other at 3 (8) double threads/cm (in.).

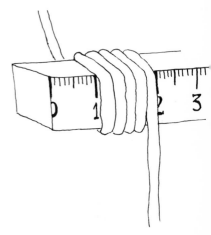

Finding the number of threads per cm (in.) by winding round a ruler

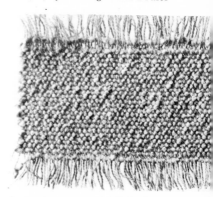

A sample on a warp at 7 single threads per cm (18 ends per inch)

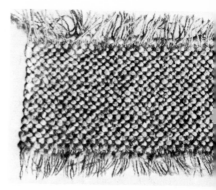

A sample on a warp at 3 double threads per cm (8 ends per inch)

23

The skein holder opens, like an
umbrella, to the size of the skein

It is held by a sliding stop, which
allows it to rotate when the screw
is tightened

Different stages in winding a bobbin

A spool rack

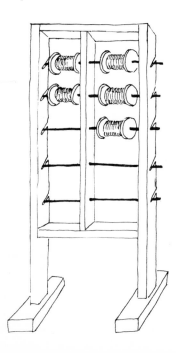

Shrinkage of the weft, contraction of the warp

When calculating the width of the warp an extra amount should be allowed for shrinkage of the cloth and 'take-up' in the width during weaving. Depending on the material and the type of batten used, the difference between the width of the warp in the reed and the finished width of the cloth can vary from 1 per cent to 12 per cent.

In calculating the length an allowance must be made for: (a) the loom wastage, at both ends of the warp, of 50 to 100 cm, ($\frac{1}{2}$ to $\frac{3}{4}$ yd), depending on the size of the loom, (b) take-up and shrinkage in the weaving, which, depending on the type of weft, can be from 1 per cent to 10 per cent of the length of the warp on the mill.

2.2 Warping

Warping is the process of laying together threads of the correct length and number to form the warp of a particular piece of cloth. The threads must all be at the same tension and must not be allowed to tangle or to be out of order. Often yarns are sold on bobbins, cops or cones; others are sold in skeins and need rewinding onto bobbins before warping can begin.

Bobbin winding

Skeins should be stretched sharply several times between the forearms to loosen the threads, before placing the skein on the skein-holder. Small bobbins can be wound on an electric bobbin winder. For longer warps, larger wooden bobbins can be used. They have to be wound by hand, but fewer of them are needed. All bobbins must be evenly wound and well tensioned.

It is advisable to have as many bobbins as there are threads per centimetre (inch) or a multiple (sub-multiple) of this number if possible, so that subsequent processes will be easier. The bobbins are placed on a spool-rack for warping.

The warping mill or frame

The warping apparatus is designed to accommodate, in a comparatively restricted space, the longest possible warp, so that an even tension can be maintained while warping. There are two main types of warping apparatus, the mill and the frame or the board[1].

(a) *The warping mill* The warping mill is a skeleton cylinder of four or more sides revolving about an axis which is usually, but not necessarily, vertical. A mill for hand weaving is usually of about 2–3 metres (yards) in circumference, and about 2 m (yd) in height. The length of the side will depend on the number of sections, and varies from 30 to 75 cm (12 in.–30 in.). Two horizontal bars, with pegs for the crosses, can be fixed anywhere in the mill between two of the verticals. The first is fastened at the top of the mill, and the second lower down, according to the length of warp required. A mill is an essential for really long warps, but it is cumbersome.

(b) *The warping frame or board*   A frame is perfectly adequate for warps of up to 15 m (yd)[2]. Two vertical members each carry a number of regularly spaced pegs. The distance between the verticals is the unit used for calculating the length of the warp. For example, to warp 10 m (yd), on a frame 75 cm ($\frac{3}{4}$ yd) wide, there would be:

$$10/0.75 = 13.3, \textit{ i.e. } 14 \text{ passes across the frame.}$$
$$10/\tfrac{3}{4} = 13\tfrac{1}{3}, \textit{ i.e. } 14 \text{ passes across the frame.}$$

The verticals should not be more than 1.50 m ($1\frac{1}{2}$ yd) apart, as the threads may sag and cause bad tension.

The pegs for the cross are mounted on the sides of the frame, and the warp is usually begun on the lower left-hand peg[3].

The process of warping

Whatever the type of mill or frame used, the principle of warping is the same, a group of threads is passed backwards and forwards between the first and last pegs. The group of threads used together is called a bout. Two bouts, *i.e.* there and back, make a portée.

The width of a warp is counted in portées, rather than in bouts or threads, at the lower end of the warp where the threads cross at the beginning of the return bout, *i.e.* the second half of the portée.

To make a warp 1 m (1 yd) wide, at 5 threads/cm (12 ends/in.), the spool rack will have 5 (4) bobbins, so that the bout will represent 1 cm ($\frac{1}{3}$ in.). The threads are tied together and looped over the first peg.

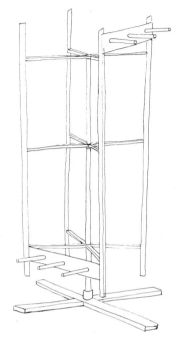

A warping mill (vertical)

Bouts crossing to form portées

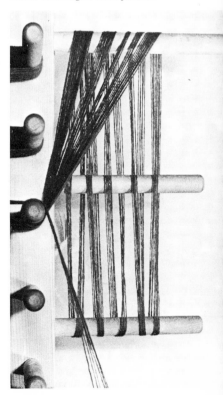

[1] On some looms the warping can be done on a sectional warp beam. The warp threads pass from the spool rack through two small sets of heddles, (the heck), to pick up the cross, and are then wound straight onto the beam. The beam is a skeleton roller, usually 1 m (1 yd) in circumference, and the warp is wound on in sections of between 2.5 and 5 cm (1–2 in.). There are two big advantages of this system: one person can handle a very large loom; the tension, controlled by a friction brake, is always constant.
[2] A warp wider than about 50 cm (20 in.) is usually made in sections of up to 30 cm (12 in.) wide.
[3] *Translater's note* British frames and warping boards have the pegs for the crosses in the top and bottom cross-members of the frame, or towards the centre of the top edge on the board. U.S. frames usually also have the pegs at the top and bottom.

A warp on a warping frame

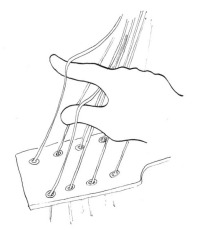

The mill is turned, or the threads are passed down the frame, until the lower set of pegs is reached. The threads are taken round the last peg and started back, and the cross formed here by the two bouts, (or half-portées), represents 2 cm ($\frac{2}{3}$ in.) of warp. A warp 1 m (1 yd) wide will need 50 (54) portées.

Counting the portées can be done only if the bouts are kept separate by forming a cross. The portée cross is made between the two lower pegs. The threads are carried over the first peg, under and round the second peg, and back under the first. This cross keeps the threads in the order in which they will be in the cloth, and permits a continuous check on the number of threads. When the warp is finished the crosses at each end are tied with cords. The cord is taken down through the cross by the end peg and back up through the other half of the cross by the second peg. The ends of the cord are tied firmly together.

Before chaining the warp, it must be made secure to maintain the evenness that it had on the mill. At the lower end of the warp, the loop round the end peg is held by knotting through it a loop of cord that will later be replaced by the stick on the warp roller of the loom. The order and tension of the threads are ensured by tying cords firmly round the whole warp at intervals of 1.5 m (1$\frac{1}{2}$ yd). These cords also act as reference marks for length.

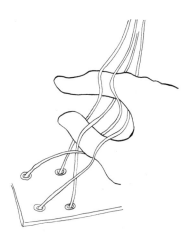

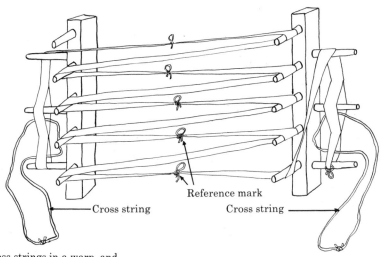

Reference mark

Cross string

Cross string

Cross strings in a warp, and
reference ties for length

The use of the paddle

So far the warp has been in bouts of one centimetre. Within each bout the threads have not been maintained in any order, and could tangle in the process of weaving. With only 5 threads/cm (12 ends/in.) this will right itself with the cross sticks and the threads will be in order by the time that they reach the heddles.

When the warp has 7 or 8 threads/cm (18–20 ends/in.) or more, a paddle is used to form a single thread cross, within each bout, at

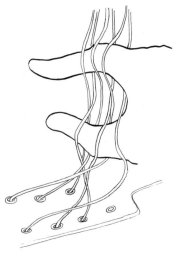

Picking up a cross with a paddle

one end of the warp. The paddle is a small thread guide with a handle and is used between the spool rack and the warping mill. The movements of the fingers are always the same during warping. The left hand holds the paddle and the bout of threads on the spool rack side of the paddle; the right hand picks up the cross. The first thread passes over the thumb and under the first finger, the second thread passes under the thumb and over the first finger[4]. When the cross has been gathered, the thumb and finger are brought together to hold the cross until it is placed on the pegs of the mill. This cross, the porrey cross, is taken at one end of the warp, the other end has the portée cross.

   To take the warp off the mill the hand is used as a crochet hook to make a large chain. (Hence the word 'chain' for warp). The chain is started at the end which will not go onto the warp roller. If a paddle has been used, this will be the end with the single thread cross (porrey cross).

---

[4] *Translator's note* In Great Britain and America the cross is usually taken up from the bottom of the paddle and not across from the side; the left hand can be used to pick up the cross when the paddle is turned round to go down the mill.

Chaining a warp

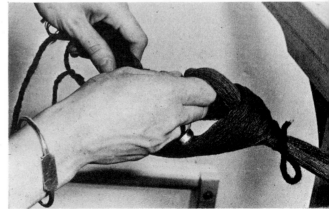
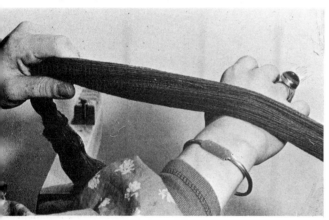

Shafts fixed in the castles

2.3 Beaming or winding

Beaming is the process of winding the warp on to the warp roller at the back of the loom, and is preceded by spreading in a raddle: a wooden frame like a very coarse reed. It has teeth of wood or metal spaced at intervals of 1 or 2 cm ($\frac{1}{2}$–1 in.). (It is quite easy to make one oneself, using large nails. The middle of a raddle is a nail, not a space). The raddle is suspended from the loom frame during beaming.

The shafts rest for the time being on 'castles', and the warp is placed across the harness, the portée cross to the back of the loom and the rest of the warp on the floor in front of the loom. After checking that the back stick is parallel to the back beam, the lacings fastening it to the back roller are slid off, the stick placed through the end loop of the warp and the lacings refastened.

The next task is to place the portées between the teeth of the raddle[5]. To balance the shafts correctly, it is important that the warp is placed centrally in the loom, particularly when the warp does not occupy the full working width of the loom.

In the example already given of a warp 1 m (1 yd) wide at 5 threads/cm (12 ends/in.), each half-portée has 5 threads (4 threads) if there are 5 (4) bobbins on the spool rack. Half the width of the warp is 25 (27) portées. To spread the warp evenly in a raddle at 2 cm ($\frac{1}{2}$ in.) spacing, one portée ($1\frac{1}{2}$) must go in each space.

Beaming is done by two people, or better still by three, if the loom is very large. One person stands a short distance away from the front

Preparing to wind the warp onto the warp beam

The back stick in the end loops of the warp

The portées being placed in the raddle

of the loom, holding a length of the warp firmly, and advances as the warp is wound onto the roller, until the hands are near the raddle. Then the next part of the chain is undone, the next warp ties taken off, the warp shaken out horizontally, checked for differences in length and the whole process repeated. The second person turns the roller by the handles on the ratchet wheel, keeping a continuous check on the warp tension generally and watching the progress of the bunches of threads through the raddle, as tangles between the portées cause broken threads. The warp wound onto the back roller must lie as evenly and as smoothly as possible.

The warp on the roller must not taper-off at the ends, or the selvedge threads will be short and break. For the whole of the first round, warp sticks the full width of the loom are placed almost side by side on top of the lacing cords, which would otherwise make the lengths of the warp threads uneven. Sticks are also inserted from time to time, three or four to a round, to prevent turns bedding into each other and to prevent the edges from slipping. It is also possible to wind in layers of strong paper with the sticks. Some warp rollers are equipped with movable flanges to hold the warp to the required width. Metal angle pieces can be wound in with the first round to serve the same purpose.

Beaming is finished when the free end of the warp is level with the beater. Although the raddle has no purpose other than to spread out the warp to the required width on the roller, it is simpler not to take it off now but to lower it slightly and use it to support the threads during threading.

The cord through the cross will give the order of the half-portées; it can be pushed back to the raddle when the threads are separated. It is replaced by the cross sticks when the warp has a single thread porrey cross[6]. All that remains to be done before threading-up is to cut the beginning of the warp, even out the threads and tie them temporarily into small bunches of a few centimetres (2–3 in.) of warp width.

2.4 Errors in warping

The first stage in dressing a loom is complete, but mistakes may have occurred:

(a) mistakes in the cross: the threads must be recounted before putting them in the raddle.
(b) mistakes in the number of portées: too few threads – a small extra warp must be made and wound on at the same time as the other; too many threads – the extra threads must be removed from the back stick and progressively discarded as the warp is wound on.

---

[5] The cord through the portée cross is not removed, either during mounting the loom or during the weaving, except at the very end. It is a guarantee; if the worst happens, the warp can always be reversed.

[6] A stick is placed in each side of the cross, odd threads over one, even threads over the other. The ends of the sticks are tied together with a strong cord.

Threading a four-shaft loom
single-handed

(c) a bout has not followed the correct path downwards or upwards on the mill or frame: if it is too long, discard it as above; if, although it is in the cross, it is short, the spool rack is placed in front of the loom and each thread in the bout is tied to a thread from a bobbin. The bout set in must always be at the same tension as the rest of the warp.

Finally the batten must be removed (and the breast beam if it is in the way), the stool placed as near to the shafts as possible and the threading can begin. If a threading hook is not available, a number 8 or 10 crochet hook can be used.

2.5 Threading

This is also called drawing-in or entering.

In the course of describing the different parts of the loom, the importance of the harness, which carries the heddles, has been mentioned.

Threading consists of passing each thread of the warp individually through one of the eyes of the heddles, following exactly the order in the weave plan and taking the threads in the order in which they are in the cross.

Threading a two-shaft harness

This is the most simple harness and can be used only for plain weave and its variations. If shaft 1 carries the first thread, shaft 2 carries the second thread, shaft 1 the third and shaft 2 the fourth, etc. All the odd threads will be on the first shaft and all the even threads will be on the second shaft. The mechanism merely raises or lowers alternately the first and then the second shaft.

Single-handed threading

Threading is generally started at the right-hand edge and threading drafts are read from right to left[7]. It is possible to begin in the middle, to make sure that the warp is central: there is certain to be as many heddles and threads on either side of the centre on each shaft.

The arrangement of shafts is always shown on the pattern draft. Swedish drafts have shaft 1 at the back, others have shaft 1 at the front[8].

The heddles are numbered according to the shafts on which they are mounted.

To thread up a plain weave on a two-shaft harness, the first heddle of the first shaft is selected. The left hand picks up, to the left of the

[7] If the pattern is symmetrical about the centre, under the draft may be written: AB, border; BC, half-repeat of the pattern. Thread straight through, then back through CB, and then BA, from left to right in the second half.
[8] *Translator's note* As it is more practical to thread looms from back to front, the shafts were always numbered, logically, from the back to the front. With the comparatively recent revival of interest in hand weaving, the drafts are now written in what is on paper the more logical way from the front to the back, except in countries such as Sweden where there is an unbroken tradition of hand weaving and the original method is retained.

The threads hanging from the raddle, ready for threading

heddle, the first thread, and with the thumb and index finger places it onto the hook inserted into the eye of the heddle by the right hand. The threads, as they are drawn through, are held in the right hand together with the hook[9]. When there are too many threads for convenience, the bunch is tied with a loop and a new bunch started.

Threading is done more quickly if four threads are held in between the fingers of the left hand and four heddles are selected at once.

Threading with two persons

One person is on a stool behind the loom – or between the harness and the back beam if the loom is very deep – and places each thread in turn on the hook which the second person, sitting in front of the loom, has passed through the eye of a heddle. The threads are taken from the cross in strict order, and are held between the thumb and index finger whilst being placed on the hook. To prevent mistakes occurring, both persons check the threading as it is being done.

Mistakes in threading are common at first; as many are not visible until the first pick of weft has been thrown, these corrections will be dealt with in a later section. There is one common fault which can be eliminated however. When threading a symmetrical design, if the end thread on the left is odd, the end thread on the right must be even, unless the draft indicates that the point of the repeat is to be doubled.

Threading with an assistant

Reading a draft

The threads of the warp, always parallel to each other, pass through the loom and perpendicularly through the shafts, where they are spread out horizontally. The diagram shows this from above the loom.

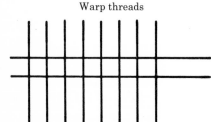

Warp threads

2 ⎫
  ⎬ Shafts
1 ⎭

[9] When the threads are very heavy, such as string or nylon, they slip back out of the heddles if they are not held.

The heddle through which a thread is entered is marked by a dot. A draft for a two-shaft plain weave is illustrated.

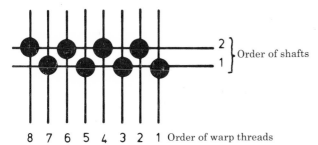

2 ⎫
1 ⎬ Order of shafts

8 7 6 5 4 3 2 1   Order of warp threads

To make the threading clearer the shafts are represented by the spaces between two lines rather than the lines themselves: this is the method adopted here.

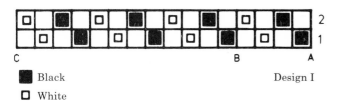

C   B   A

2
1

Design I

■ Black

□ White

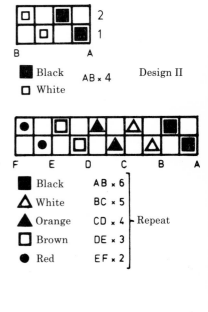

□ ■ 2
□ ■ 1

B   A

■ Black   AB × 4   Design II
□ White

● □ ▲ △ ■
● □ ▲ △ ■

F   E   D   C   B   A

■ Black   AB × 6 ⎫
△ White   BC × 5 ⎪
▲ Orange   CD × 4 ⎬ Repeat
□ Brown   DE × 3 ⎪
● Red   EF × 2 ⎭

The order of the letters A, B, indicates that the draft is read from right to left. The letters are a check to avoid threading incorrect repeats. Design I could be reduced to design II. When the warp is striped, the repeats are indicated by using different symbols for each colour.

Threading a harness of more than two shafts

The method is the same. The draft shows in which order the threads pass through the shafts. The threading is the interaction of the warp with the shafts; the greater the number of shafts, the greater the possibilities in the weaving. The variations of threading are infinite; each alteration creates a new fabric which can be diversified even further with the weft.

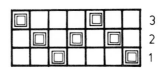

3
2
1

Design I

3
2
1

Design II

2.6 Threading the reed or 'sleying'

The reed spreads out the warp to its correct width. The batten must be replaced in the loom, putting in the reed of the correct number of threads/cm (ends/in.) at the same time.

Threading the reed is done with a flat 'reed hook', held in the right hand when working towards the left and vice versa. The threading can be done either standing or sitting down. The hand holding the hook also holds the threads drawn through the reed to prevent their

Reed hook. It can be made out of metal, bone, plastic or card

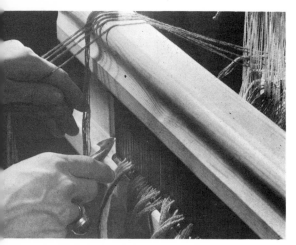

Each thread goes through a dent in the reed

The threads must be taken in the order in which they are in the heddles

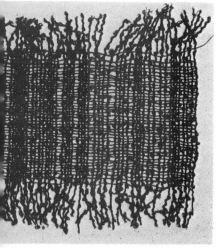

Stripes made by irregular threading in the reed

slipping back. The other hand holds the threads in the first four heddles. The hand is closed to hold the threads in order and is placed behind the reed facing the hand which holds the reed hook. Attention must be concentrated on the front of the reed so that dents will not be missed or doubled: the hand behind the reed holds the threads in order, so that there is no need to watch them. Each bunch of threads is retied with a loop in front of the reed as it is finished.

Usually the threading of the reed is even. Irregular threadings create new fabrics, but they must be planned in advance to calculate the number of threads in the warp and the distribution in the raddle. The threading of the warp in the reed influences the spacing of the heddles on the shafts.

The reed not only serves as a guide to the shuttle, it also is used, in the batten, to beat-up the weft.

The working of each thread is determined by the heddles, and its position in the warp by the reed. The warp can now be tied on to the front roller of the loom.

2.7 Tying on the warp

It is necessary to remove everything that may hinder the accurate tensioning of the warp; the raddle, the cross strings, the castles supporting the shafts, and to check that the front stick is parallel to the breast beam. There are several ways of tying on the warp; two are described here.

(a) Undo a bunch of threads, comb it out to equalise the tension, take it over the stick, back underneath, bring the two halves up to the top again outside the original bunch and tie them on top. The warp tension must be kept constant, so bunches are taken from the centre

36

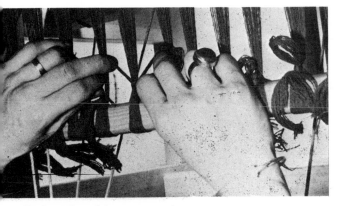

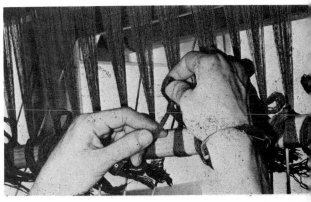

Each section of the warp must be
at the same tension

When the tension is right, the knot
is finished with a bow

of the warp or from one or other of the selvedges alternately. This
method is particularly useful when a warp fringe is planned.

(b) Comb out a bunch of warp threads and tie a knot firmly in the
ends. Tie a long cord to one end of the front stick, and take it round
and round the stick, passing through a bunch of threads, above the
knot, each time.

The tension is good, the loss at the beginning of the warp is only
a few centimetres (2 or 3 in.).

Irregular tension will not right itself, but becomes worse as the
weaving progresses, until finally it causes mistakes in the weaving.
Threads too tight or too loose will distort the cloth.

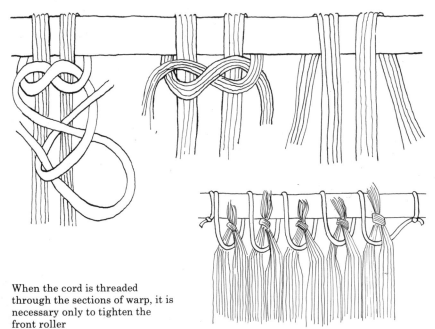

Stages in tying the warp onto the
front stick

When the cord is threaded
through the sections of warp, it is
necessary only to tighten the
front roller

3 Reading a draft: treadling drafts and weave plans

3.1 The treadling draft

The draft has a direct connection with the threading used.

Taking the two-shaft plain weave again as an example, the threading draft will be this.

Each of the shafts must rise and fall alternately.

The mechanism of the treadles has been explained in the first chapter, therefore it will be assumed that shaft 1, through the marches or countermarches, is tied to treadle 1, and shaft 2 to treadle 2. According to the type of loom, the shaft may either rise or sink when the treadle is pressed.

This is shown quite simply diagrammatically.

Order of treadles

Order of shafts

As the threading is inseparable from the tie-up, both are shown on the same diagram.

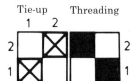

Tie-up   Threading

The next diagram shows some of the different ways of tying up the treadles using the same threading draft. (The weave is a simple four-shaft twill. Each shaft carries the same number of heddles.)

Example 1 is the simplest tie-up, a plain weave. Shafts 1 and 3 are tied to treadle 1, shafts 2 and 4 to treadle 2.

In example 2 each shaft is independent. Raising or lowering the shafts in order, 1 to 4, will give a straight twill, weft-faced or warp-faced respectively.

In example 3 each treadle operates two shafts, and by treadling in order, the shafts are operated progressively in pairs, 1 2, 2 3, 3 4, 4 1, then repeat.

Example 4 combines the twill and plain weave tie-ups. The most useful tie-up is number 2. Using single treadles in order 1, 2, 3, 4, gives a warp- or weft-faced twill. For a balanced twill or a plain weave, two treadles are depressed simultaneously, 1 2, 2 3, 3 4, 4 1, for a balanced twill; 1 3, 2 4, for a plain weave.

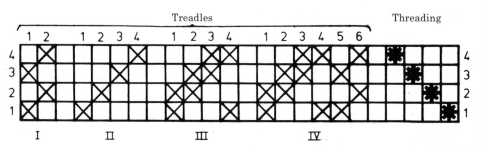

3.2 Weaves

A balanced twill, woven on a sinking shed loom, is taken as an example.

In the weave plan, as distinct from the threading draft and the lifting plan or treadling draft, the black (solid) squares show warp threads on top of weft threads and the white (hollow) squares the opposite. Each vertical row of squares represents a warp thread or 'end' and each horizontal row represents a weft thread or 'pick'. The solid triangles are the tie-up, and the open triangles are the treadling drafts. There are only three fundamental weaves, all the others are variations of them.

(a) *Plain weave* Plain weave or 'tabby' has a number of different names, according to the material being woven; calico or poplin for cotton, alpaca for a wool lustre, taffeta for silk.

It is the most simple weave. The odd and even ends rise and fall successively, covering the weft threads. The weave is completely balanced and has no right or wrong side.

The minimum number of warp and weft threads for one repeat of the weave is two ends of warp and two picks of weft.

(b) *Twill* Twill is a weave and not a fabric. The cloth shows diagonal lines to the left or to the right because the threads do not rise and fall alternately 1 up and 1 down, *i.e.* 1&1, but 1&2, 1&3, 1&4, 2&2, 2&3, 2&4, 3&3, 3&4, etc. The weft passes under one warp end and then over two, three, four, etc. At each 'pick' of weft the 'float' of weft moves sideways one warp thread. The fabric has a right and a wrong side when is an unequal number of threads rising and sinking. The balanced twills 2&2, 3&3, 4&4, etc., do not therefore have a right and a wrong side[10].

The minimum number of threads for a twill weave is three ends and picks.

(c) *Satin weave* The satin weave makes a cloth with a smooth surface. One set of threads covers the other almost completely. It is called warp faced or weft faced depending on which set of threads predominates. The move or step sideways of the float is always more than one or the weave would be a twill.

The minimum number of threads for a satin weave is five ends and picks. A good irregular satin can be woven on four ends and picks.

It is always possible to work out the threading and treadling from a weave plan.

Point paper designs

A weave plan is constructed from a sample of cloth with the aid of a 'linen prover', a small magnifying glass mounted on a base with an exactly square aperture having graduated sides.

[10] *Translator's note* Balanced twills have a right and a wrong side on some fabrics. With fine, hard yarns spun in opposite directions for warp and weft, the threads will tend to stand off each other in the finished cloth, and a twill running *against* the surface direction of the fibres will be thrown into prominence. When such a fabric is turned over onto the back, the direction of twist of the yarns will not alter, but the angle of the twill is reversed and will now run *with* the surface direction of the fibres and so be subdued.

Complete diagram of a 2&2 twill

Weave diagrams

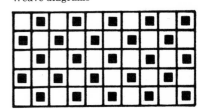

Plain

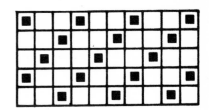

Twill

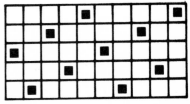

Satin

On point páper (graph paper) a square is drawn to represent the part of the specimen seen in the linen prover. The first horizontal row of squares on the paper corresponds to the first thread of weft in the cloth, the first vertical column to the first warp thread. Each time a warp thread crosses over a weft thread, the square representing the intersection is filled in in black; where the weft passes over the warp, the square is left blank.

Construction of threading and treadling drafts from a weave plan

A frame is drawn above the weave plan; in this will be drawn the threading draft. The tie-up and treadling draft will be drawn on the left. Each warp end is followed through upwards and a mark is placed on one or other of the shafts to show on which one it is threaded. Successive ends are placed on successive shafts in order, working from shaft 1 to shaft 4. Ends which work the same are carried on the same shaft. To the side of the weave plan, the vertical columns now represent the treadles, and, in a similar way to the threading, each different pick of weft is given to a different treadle. The tie-up is drawn where the columns of treadles cross the rows of shafts. Where, for instance, warp ends 1 and 2 are below the weft, treadle 1 is tied to shafts 1 and 2 on a sinking shed loom. (The tie-up and treadling are drawn as frequently on the right of the weave plan as on the left nowadays.)

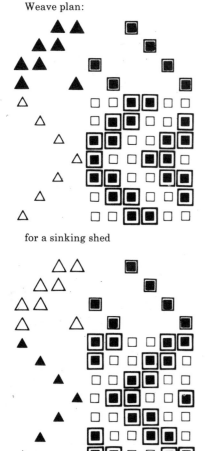

Weave plan:

for a sinking shed

for a rising shed

Drafting threading, tie-up and treadling from a weave plan

The difference between drafts for rising shed and sinking shed looms

In the previous draft, the black squares (marks) represented warp up, white squares (blanks) weft up. Threads 1 and 2 were covered by the first pick of weft, therefore as treadle 1 must have lowered shafts 1 and 2 for that pick, the draft is for a sinking shed loom.

If shafts 1 and 2 had to rise when treadle 1 was depressed, on this loom shafts 3 and 4 would be tied to that treadle, shafts 4 and 1 to treadle 2, 1 and 2 to treadle 3, and 2 and 3 to treadle 4. The order of treadling could have been changed, treadling 3, 4, 1, 2, instead of 1, 2, 3, 4.

40

3.3 Tying up the treadles

This is done each time that a new warp is threaded on the loom, to ensure that the mounting is well adjusted.

After the warp has been beamed, threaded through the heddles and the reed and tied on, the mounting can be tied on and adjusted. The work is done from the top downwards, using a good quality loom cord.

The line of the warp is the starting point, and this determines the height of the shafts, which are tied directly to the rockers on a countermarch loom or to the pulleys or heddle-horses on a two-shaft or a four-shaft counterbalanced loom respectively. When the cord is doubled, the best knot to use is the lark's head. (See p. 42). On a countermarch loom the rockers must be locked with the pin or bar before tying the mounting. On a counterbalanced loom the shafts must be slung at the correct height from the side frame. On both types of loom the shafts must always be horizontal and level with each other at this stage.

The marches or lamms and the countermarches must also be horizontal. They are tied to the treadles, according to the pattern, with double cords using snitch knots (see p. 42). One treadle may sink one, two or three shafts together at the same time, depending on the pattern.

The sketch shows a 2&2 twill tied up on a counterbalanced loom (A) and a countermarch loom (B).

The countermarches or lamms are tied to the bottom shaft stick, and the marches to the top shaft stick via the rockers.

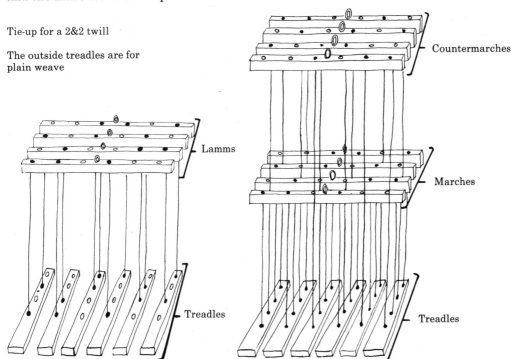

Tie-up for a 2&2 twill

The outside treadles are for plain weave

Countermarches

Lamms

Marches

Treadles

Treadles

A on a counterbalanced loom

B on a countermarch loom

3.4 Knots

Snitch knot (1). This is a very important knot in weaving when an adjustable tie between two levers is needed. Make a lark's head in the loop from the treadles, and insert the two ends from the lamms or the countermarches above. Finish with half a reef knot (or two half-hitches).

Lark's head knot or cow hitch (2).

Figure-of-eight loop knot (3). This knot, or the overhand loop knot, is tied temporarily in a bunch of threads to stop it from slipping back through the reed or heddles.

Granny knot (4). The only use of the granny knot is for tying the eyes in string heddles.

Reef knot (5).

Weaver's knot (6).

Read from left to right

1 & 2 Snitch knot (step 2 is a lark's head)

3 Loop knot

4 Granny knot

5 Reef knot

6 Weaver's knot

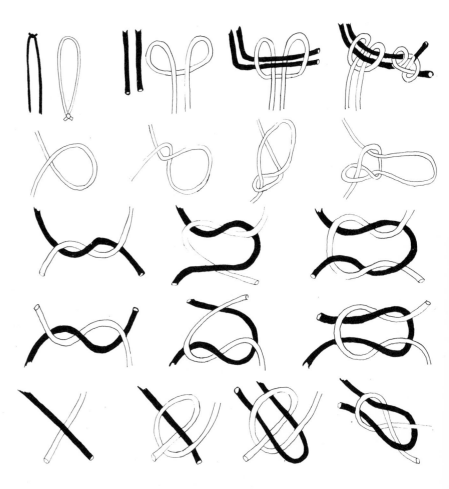

4 Beginning the weaving

4.1 Preparing the bobbins

The bobbin must be small enough to go comfortably in the shuttle and unwind without jamming. It must be firmly wound with the threads lying in an even spiral.

Pirns for flying shuttles

The pirn is a conical type of bobbin which does not rotate, but which unwinds over the end, so therefore the eye of a pirn shuttle is near one end of the shuttle cavity. The pirn is wound on a tube of stiff cardboard or wood, using either a hand or an electric bobbin winder.

Bobbins for roller shuttles

The bobbin rotates on the spindle and the thread unwinds from the side, so the eye of the shuttle is in the middle of the cavity. The thread is wound evenly on both ends of the bobbin, usually on a wooden bobbin or on a tube of rolled-up paper. The diagrams show successive stages in the making of a bobbin. A circular disc, with the diameter less than the length of the bobbin cavity, is cut from a sheet of strong paper, (e.g. good brown wrapping paper), and then wound onto the spindle of the bobbin winder. As the spindle is slightly tapered, the paper bobbin or 'quill' grips tightly after the first turn or so of thread.

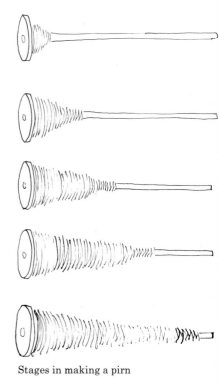

Stages in making a pirn

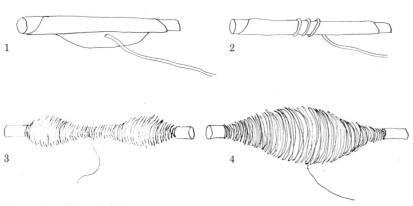

Stages in making a bobbin on a paper 'quill' for a roller shuttle

4.2 The first rows of weaving

The cross sticks

A pair of cross sticks must be put in the warp to keep the threads in order. The two plain weave sheds are raised one after the other, and in each shed a cross stick is placed at the back of the heddles. The threads are separated carefully behind the cross sticks, and the sticks are worked along the warp to the back beam of the loom. The sticks are moved back in a similar manner every time that they hinder the movement of the heddles, i.e. every 30 to 60 cm (1 to 2 ft) of weaving, depending on the depth of the loom.

Cross sticks in the warp

Removing spare heddles

Empty heddles at the ends of the shafts should be removed and the safety cords retied to prevent loose heddles damaging the selvedge during weaving.

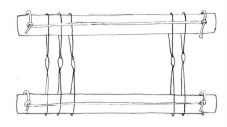
The safety cord on the shaft stick

The tension

If the knots at the beginning of the warp are too close to the reed, a short length of warp must be let off the back roller, wound forward and retensioned with the front roller. The exact amount of tension depends on the strength of the warp and on the design of the cloth. A tight warp gives a better shed, allowing the shuttle to pass through more easily, and the weave is more clear-cut.

The warp should always be slackened off whenever the loom is left for more than a short time, so that the threads do not loose their elasticity.

The first few centimetres

The 'heading', at the beginning of the work, is woven with a weft of a strongly contrasting colour to check for any mistakes that may have occurred in the threading through the heddles and the reed.

(a) *errors in threading the heddles*   They are usually quite obvious; when two threads work together as if in the same heddle, the weave looks like this:

Instead of the threading being 1, 2, 3, 4, 1, 2, 3, 4, it is probable that it is 1, 2, 3, 4, 4, 3, 2, 1, or 4, 3, 2, 1, 1, 2, 3, 4, if the mistake has occurred in the centre of the warp and the threading has been done both ways from the middle outwards. The only remedy is to cut the extra thread, which will then hang down from the back beam, and rethread the reed to the nearest selvedge. If two threads are doubled anywhere else except at the centre, the heddles as well as the reed will have to be rethreaded.

When three threads work together, the weave looks like this:

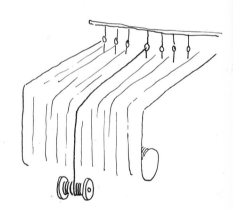

The number of threads is correct, but the threading of the repeat is faulty. One shaft has been omitted and another doubled, giving a threading such as 1, 1, 3, 4, or 1, 2, 2, 4. The mistake is corrected by inserting a new heddle in the right place, taking the offending thread out of the old heddle and re-threading through the new heddle and the reed. The new heddle is put on the shaft by undoing the knot at the top, sliding it along the bottom shaft stick through the loops of the other heddles and then re-tying it with a granny knot at the top in its correct place.

Joining a warp thread

45

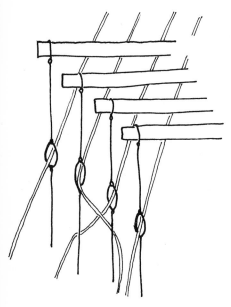

Threading mistake: crossing two threads in the heddles

When a thread is missing completely, a new length of warp thread is wound onto a heavy bobbin, threaded through a new heddle, which had been placed in the harness as before, threaded through the reed and then wound round a pin in the heading.

If a warp thread does not weave in, it has been crossed with another in the threading. The threads must be untied, taken out and re-threaded through the heddles and the reed.

When the mistake is in the pattern the whole of the warp from the mistake onwards must be re-threaded.

If there is one thread which does not shed well one way, either up or down, it may have gone below or above, instead of through, the eye of the heddle.

If one shaft will not rise and fall properly, it will probably be due to a heddle from the next shaft having caught on the end of one of the sticks of the shaft which is not working well.

(b) *Errors in threading the reed* Threads are often crossed in the reed, but this mistake is obvious and soon corrected.

If two threads are in the same dent, or a dent has been missed, the reed must be re-threaded from the mistake to the nearest selvedge.

(c) *Errors in tension* If the cloth is crammed in some places and open in others, then sections of the warp are at different tensions, and the knots need re-tying.

These apparently small corrections may appear to be a nuisance, after such a long preparation, but they must not be evaded. A mistake in the reed will make a light or a heavy streak the whole length of the cloth. Bad tension in the warp will distort the cloth and make it unusable.

(d) *Errors in the adjustment of the loom* A poor shed is often due to a batten set at the wrong height, preventing the threads from moving far enough. The warp threads should be set in the middle of the reed on a counterbalanced loom, low for a rising shed and high for a sinking shed loom, to obtain the correct opening.

If the treadles touch the floor before the shed is fully opened, then the bottom ties must be readjusted (the ties from the treadles to the lamms or the marches).

If the apron or the cords from the cloth roller are in the way of the weaver's knees, the apron (or cord) has been taken round the wrong side of the knee beam. In some looms the knee beam can be taken out, the warp slackened off and the beam put back below the apron or cords. If this is not possible, the warp knots will have to be undone and the tying on started again.

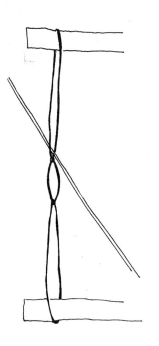

Threading mistake: thread through the doup instead of the eye of a heddle

4.3 The process of weaving

The first rows of weaving

The first row is critical. Whenever possible, the shuttle should be thrown towards the side on which the treadle is depressed. The whole body leans towards the side to apply pressure on the treadle, and it is easier and more natural to throw the shuttle towards this side as well. It is important to acquire this rhythm of leaning and throwing to the same side. It also gives a second check on the correct treadle to use when restarting weaving after a break. If the shuttle is on the right the left foot will be used first.

When the shuttle is in the right hand, the left hand pushes the batten back from the cloth towards the heddles. The shuttle, held with the thumb on the top, first finger on the nose of the shuttle and the remaining fingers underneath, is thrown with a flick of the wrist and the forefinger into the shed and is caught between the thumb and fingers of the left hand, which is against the shuttle race ready to receive it and is holding back the batten at the same time. The right hand does not stop when the shuttle is released but continues on to the middle of the batten, and as soon as the shuttle is clear swings the batten forward to beat-up the pick of weft into place. The right foot now depresses the second treadle and the left hand returns the shuttle across to the right and beats-up the new row of weft.

The exact timing of the beat is important. If the shed is changed *before* the beat, the weft is trapped by the crossing of the warp and shows up more on the surface of the cloth. This is beating on a closed shed and is used for weft-faced cloths. Beating on an open shed, with the shed changed *after* the beat while the reed is held against the fell of the cloth, causes the warp threads to lie evenly in the cloth and gives a better balanced structure. This is used for firm cloths.

During beating up, the hand holding the shuttle stays near the cloth, so that as little weft as possible is drawn off the bobbin. When the shuttle is thrown again, the slight tension on the weft as the bobbin starts to unwind pulls the slack into the shed and gives a firm selvedge. The speed of the shuttle lays the weft in at an even tension, and there should be no need to touch the weft at all. If there is any slack present, the bobbin can be checked with the third finger from underneath the shuttle while the slack is taken up by moving the shuttle.

This is a seemingly complicated explanation of what is basically a simple series of movements. It is most important for the beginner to go through the sequence slowly and rhythmically, and not to try to go too fast. A slow, deliberate and connected series of actions will develop rhythm, and very soon speed, without sacrificing quality. A series of quick, jerky, disconnected actions will never become fast, and the quality of the cloth will suffer. The beat may be light or heavy, but must always be even to make a good cloth.

The selvedges

The last 5 or 6 mm ($\frac{1}{4}$ in.) of warp at the edges of the cloth should always be a little firmer than the main cloth to provide a strong

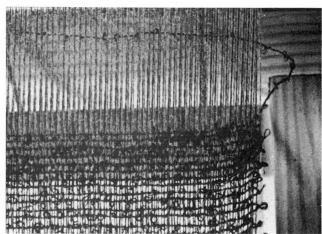

Selvedges in an open cloth woven
with a slack weft

selvedge. The last 3 or 4 threads can be doubled in heddles and reed,
or set singly in the heddles and double in the reed. The slight pull-in
during weaving of about 2 or 3 cm (1–1½ in.) overall is allowed for
when calculating the width of the warp and helps to create a good
edge, but too much will cause fraying and broken threads.

Exceptionally, in a very open cloth, selvedges may be left as open
as the main warp. In this case, a length of weft has to be unwound
from the bobbin *before* throwing, by pulling the arm back away
from the cloth whilst beating the previous row, and the beat must
always be on an open shed. The 'reediness', which will not be
removed by an open-shed beat, can be seen in the photographs on
this page, though in a cloth as open as this it tends to disappear in the
finishing. This type of selvedge is not as strong as the usual selvedges,
but is more supple.

The batten
The batten must always be held centrally when beating-up, so that
each row of weft is laid parallel to the previous rows. An off-centre
beat will compress one side more than another and make light or
dark streaks in the cloth.

Winding on
The cloth is wound onto the front roller at intervals, and warp sticks
or strong paper can be wound in to keep the tension even. For long
warps, a small piece of brightly coloured thread can be looped round
the end selvedge thread every 50 or 100 cms (½ or 1 yd) as a continuous
check on the length. This saves having to unwind the cloth at a later
stage to measure the amount woven and then re-wind it, which is
difficult to do without spoiling the tension.

Joining the weft
When a bobbin runs out, a join is made at the end of one row or the
beginning of the next. The beginning of the new thread overlaps the
end of the old one for about 2–3 cm (¾–1 in.) in the same shed. A knot
in the weft is cut out and the ends overlapped in the same way.

48

Colours are changed in a cloth with narrow stripes by carrying the threads up the selvedge from one stripe to the next. With wide stripes, the weft is cut off and the new colour overlapped with the previous colour as if it were an ordinary weft join.

4.4 Accidents in weaving

A broken warp thread
The thread is removed from the heddle, and a new length of the same thread is tied with a bow to the old thread near the back of the loom. The old thread is left hanging down and a new length is threaded through heddles and reed woven in with a needle alongside the original end in the cloth for about 2–3 cm ($\frac{3}{4}$–1 in.) and finally wound round a pin to hold it (see diagram page 45). When the cloth has been woven far enough for the hanging thread to reach the cloth, the bow is untied, the old thread replaced, woven in with a needle and wound round the pin again. Knots are never left in the weaving.

Backweaving
A few centimetres in from the selvedge, pull two warp threads apart and cut the weft threads exposed between them. Part the same threads again and continue cutting the weft back to the mistake. Repeat at the other selvedge, then treadle in the reverse order and pull out the cut yarns from the centre. If the weft sticks in the warp too much, make a further cut or cuts nearer the centre.

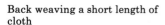

Back weaving a short length of cloth

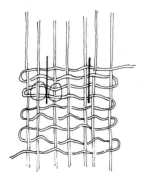

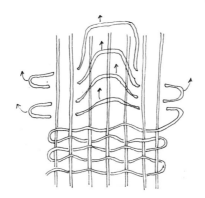

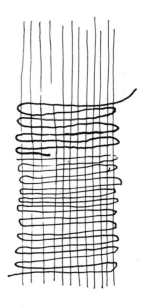

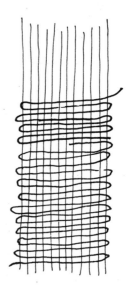

Change of colour in the weft

4.5 Weaving with a flying shuttle

The right hand holds the picking stick, the left hand the batten. The batten is pushed back, the right hand pulls the cord which throws the shuttle and the left hand beats up. The feet stay on the treadles as the weaving is very fast.

5 Finishes

When, near the end of the warp, the back stick has appeared over the back beam of the loom, the cross sticks are removed and the weaving can continue until the back stick is so close to the heddles that they cannot move enough to make a shed. Then the warp is slackened off by releasing the catch on the warp roller, the shafts tied to the top of the loom or the pegs put in the jacks on a countermarch loom and the warp is cut off in front of the reed, or, if a fringe is wanted, along the back stick behind the harness. Then the front roller is released and the length of cloth unwound. The front knots are either cut or untied.

Despite all the care taken, almost inevitably there will be faults which require attention. The cloth is spread flat on a table and checked on both sides. When a thread has not worked normally, it is cut at one end of the fault, withdrawn and then woven in with a needle as if for a join.

The end of the warp can be sewn or fringed.

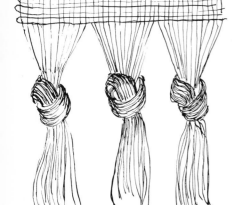

5.1 Fringes

Fringes can be very varied:
    simple fringe
    double-knotted fringe
    plaited fringe
    loop-knotted fringe
Fringes on the selvedges are crocheted or knotted with short lengths of yarn.

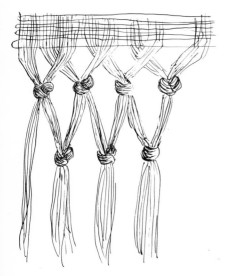

Straight fringe

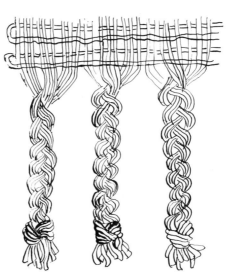

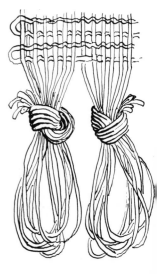

Double-knotted fringe

Plaited fringe

Looped fringe

5.2 Woven fringes lengthways

The loom needs to be considerably wider than the cloth. Eight strong extra threads are warped on each side of the main warp. They are wound on, threaded and sleyed as usual, but at least 12–15 cm (5–6 in.) outside the main warp. The loops at the edge are cut as the weaving progresses, every time that the warp is wound on.

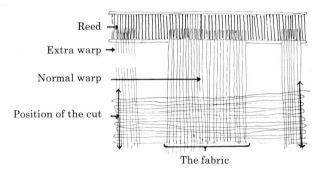

Weaving a fabric with a fringe on 4 sides

5.3 Cutting a long length

The ends of the cloth will unravel by an amount which can be quite considerable, depending on the type of materials used. This can be prevented by running a row or two of fine machine stitching across the cloth as soon as it is off the loom. If the length has to be cut, two double rows are stitched across the cloth about 1 cm ($\frac{1}{2}$ in.) apart and the cloth cut between them.

5.4 Sizing a warp

A light dressing of size does not harm the warp, but gives it a slight stiffness and smoothness which makes the weaving much easier.

Recipe for size with 1 litre of water $1\frac{3}{4}$ pints
Mix together: 50 g flour or starch $1\frac{5}{8}$ oz
             2 g wax or glycerine   1/20 oz
             1 g copper sulphate   1/40 oz
        (to inhibit the growth of mould)
             1 litre water $1\frac{3}{4}$ pints
Boil and simmer well.

Spray or paint the size on the warp, either on the warping mill or during winding on.

Basic examples

1 Two-shaft Weaving

Two-shaft weaving is the oldest type of all. The principle is very simple, similar to darning. Two sets of threads cross each other at right-angles; the first set is stretched on the loom and the second set is woven across from side to side, one thread at a time, under all the odd threads one way and under all the even threads the other way.

A home-made frame loom

A frame loom has to be at least as wide as the proposed weaving, and slightly longer. The two end pieces must be stronger and heavier than the side pieces. Both the end pieces carry two rows of nails, each spaced at 1 cm ($\frac{1}{2}$ in.) intervals, the second row about 1 cm ($\frac{1}{2}$ in.) behind, and in the spaces of, the first. The warp thread goes backwards and forwards from one end of the loom to the other. This will give a warp of about two ends per centimetre, (4 ends/inch). For a heavier sett, the warp can be taken round every nail, or three staggered rows of nails can be used. A simple shaft can be made from a piece of dowelling and some thick cotton. The threads which do not go through the loops, i.e. every other thread, pass over a thick cross stick. The weft is placed in by hand using small balls of yarn, or by using a flat stick shuttle. An ordinary comb or a small fork can be used for beating.

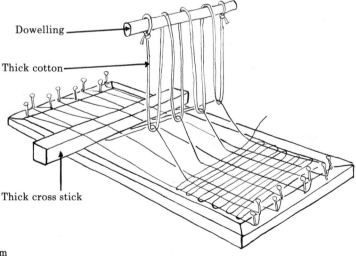

Dowelling

Thick cotton

Thick cross stick

Frame loom

52

A rigid heddle for a back-strap loom

This is a small heddle and reed combined, and can be bought from educational suppliers, but it is possible to make one. It is useful for weaving braids, belts, ties, etc. Make a warp and cut one end. The threads are passed in order through an eye and a slot ('dent') alternately. One end of the warp is knotted round something firm and the other tied to a belt or strong string tied round the waist. Leaning back tightens the warp.

During the weaving the threads in the dents do not move, those in the eyes are alternately above and below them, as the heddle is raised and lowered.

Rigid heddle

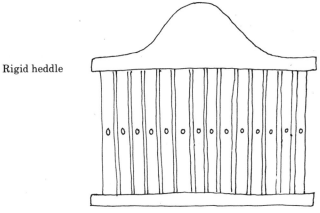

Examples

In the description of the examples which follow, the information given about the yarns is always indefinite, as each sample can be woven in several different ways.

1 Plain warp, raised weft stripes. Pattern for rugs and heavy woollen fabrics
warp rough-spun unbleached wool
weft fine natural wool
reed 30/10 (8s)
threading plain, single in heddles and reed
weaving $\left.\begin{matrix} 1 \\ 2 \end{matrix}\right\}$ × 4 rough wool

$\left.\begin{matrix} 1 \\ 2 \end{matrix}\right\}$ × 4 fine wool

$\left.\begin{matrix} 1 \\ 2 \end{matrix}\right\}$ × 2 rough wool

heavy stripes

$\left.\begin{matrix} 1 \\ 2 \end{matrix}\right\}$ × 1 rough wool

1 × 1 fine wool double

$\left.\begin{matrix} 2 \\ 1 \end{matrix}\right\}$ × 1 rough wool

. . . etc.,

Tie-up Threading

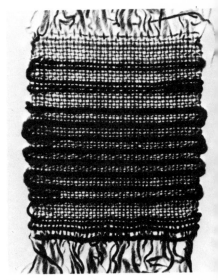

The weave is simple so that the interest can be mainly in colour and texture

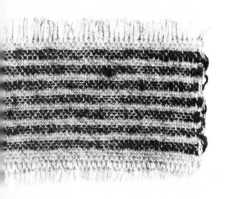

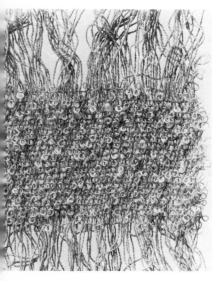

The texture of a cloth depends on the distribution of the warp and weft. In this sample a light sett gives a flexible cloth

Weft stripes need several shuttles

2 Plain warp, striped weft. Cushion cover fabric

warp fine unbleached wool singles
weft ground as warp,
      stripes in fine wool, orange and violet
reed 60/10 (15s)
threading plain, single
weaving $\left.\begin{array}{l}1\\2\end{array}\right\}$ ×1 wool ground
    1 violet wool
    2 orange wool
    1 violet wool
    $\left.\begin{array}{l}2\\1\end{array}\right\}$ ×1 wool ground
    2 orange wool
    1 violet wool
    2 orange wool
    $\left.\begin{array}{l}1\\2\end{array}\right\}$ ×1 wool ground

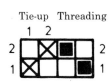

3 Textured material in natural colours. Simple warp, bouclé weft

warp fine unbleached wool
weft natural mohair loop yarn
reed 50/10 (12s)
threading single or double
weaving plain with a light beat on an open shed.

4 Tufted weaving for cushions, checked rugs, panels

The self-coloured design in uncut pile is worked in loops of weft. The design is drawn on squared paper and is interpreted freely in the weaving. The vertical columns represent warp threads, the horizontal rows the weft.

warp fine unbleached wool
weft ground, fine unbleached wool
    pattern, thick unbleached wool
reed 60/10 (15s)
weaving start with a plain cross-border to enhance the texture of the design. (1, 2, 1, 2 . . .).

The pattern weft alternates with the ground weft:
Row 1 pattern weft. Where the design has to appear, small regular loops are pulled up with the fingers between each thread, or, if this is too tight, between each pair of threads.
Row 2 ground weft
Row 3 pattern weft
To subdue the vertical lines which appear in the background, two rows of ground weft can be woven between each pattern weft.

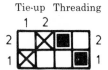

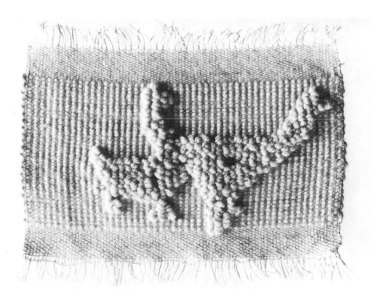

5 Weaving with two shuttles

One shuttle carries the ground weft, the other the pattern weft.

The ground threads always weave plain, under the odd threads one way, the even threads the other.

Row 1 the ground weft is passed from right to left, treadle 1

Row 2 the pattern weft also goes from right to left

Row 3 the ground weft is crossed over the pattern weft and returns from the left to right, treadle 2

Row 4 pattern weft

There are two important points to watch:

(a) there must always be a row of ground between each pair of pattern rows to tie in the warp ends.

(b) the ground treadle to be used is always the one on the opposite side to the ground shuttle, i.e. if the shuttle is on the left, the right treadle must be used and vice versa. This must become automatic, so that the full attention can be given to weaving the pattern.

The shuttles both start from the same side so that the weft threads cross only every other row

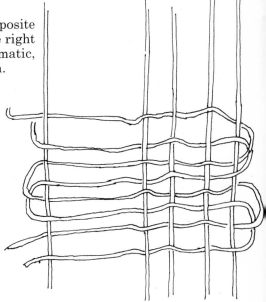

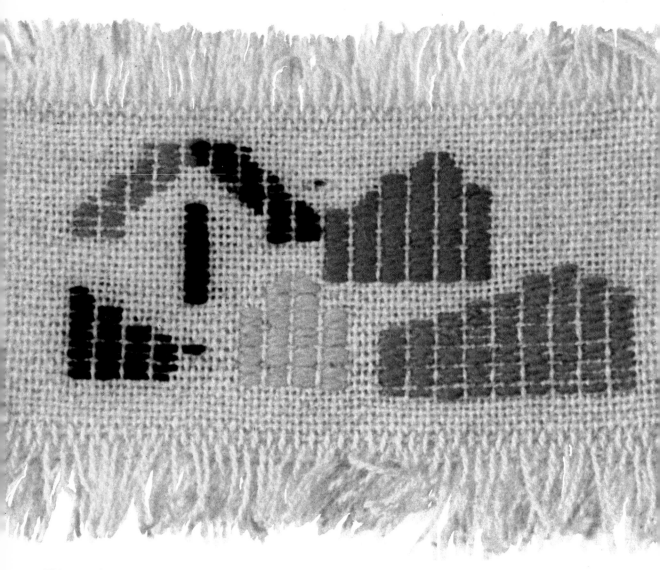

This type of weaving is very close
to needle-woven tapestry

6   Inlay weave, (Swedish dukagång), wool on a woollen ground
The design is drawn to scale on squared paper; one square represents
3, 4, 5 threads of warp. The weaving is done with at least two shuttles,
one each for the pattern and the ground. If the design includes more
than one colour, there will be as many extra shuttles as there are
additional colours.

The design is woven by passing the shuttle under one thread, over
3, 4, 5 threads, under one, over 3, 4, 5. . . .

warp fine wool
weft fine wool for the ground
    assorted wools for the pattern wefts

56

weaving 1 ground weft
        pattern weft in the same shed
      2 ground weft only
      1 ground and pattern
      2 ground only . . .

Tie-up   Threading

7 Irregular warp stripes, plain weft

warp fine wool in three colours
weft plain in one of the warp colours
reed 60/10 (15s)
threading single, the draft gives the first half of the pattern, reverse
        for the second half. (110 threads in one repeat)

The warp is striped on the mill.
Each change of colour necessitates
a change of bobbins on the spool
rack

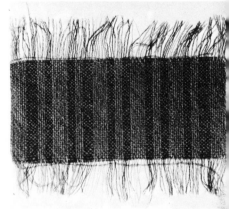

■ Fuchsia
△ Plum
▲ Red

Threading

Start

Tie-up

8 Regular warp stripes, plain weft. Pattern for a bag

warp irregular wool, two tones
weft thick wool, different colour from that of the warp
reed 40/10 (10s)
threading single or double, AB × 2, BC × 2 (minimum of 8 threads to
        one repeat)
weaving plain weave, heavy beat on an open shed

Tie-up   Threading
  1 2

■ Dark
□ Light

To weave regular squares, throw
four rows of each colour, four
light, four dark

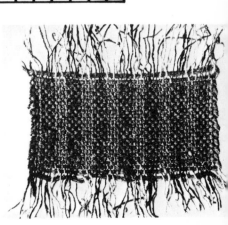

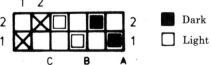

The weft can be beaten irregularly to enhance the effect of lightness

9 Warp stripes due to irregular threading in the reed. Pattern for light curtain

warp fine linen in several tones
weft irregular natural linen
reed 80/10 (20s)
threading plain in the heddles, irregular in the reed. Every 2–3 cm ($\frac{1}{2}$–1 in.) a short section of the reed is left empty (about 1.5–3 cm, $\frac{1}{2}$–1 in.). The open threading has to be allowed for in the warping and winding on
weaving plain, light beat on a closed shed

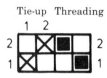

Tie-up Threading

10 Stripes in the warp and weft. Patterns for checks and plaids

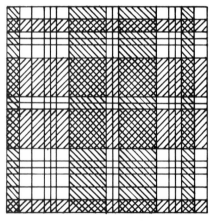

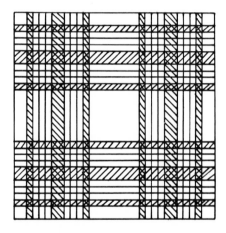

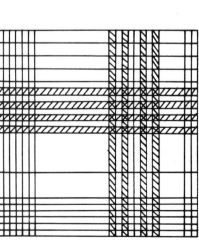

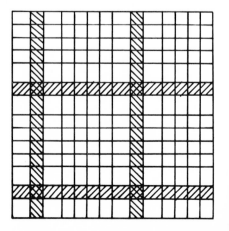

There is an endless variety of checks and tartans. The weft colours repeat those of the warp

11 Variation of plain weave, textured effect

warp fine linen
weft cotton boucle
reed 40/10 (10s)
threading as draft, one thread per heddle and dent in the reed. 56
threads per repeat
weaving $\left.\begin{matrix} 1 \\ 2 \end{matrix}\right\}$ × 4 plain weave, single weft $\left.\begin{matrix} \\ \end{matrix}\right\}$ repeat
$\left.\begin{matrix} 1 \\ 2 \end{matrix}\right\}$ × 1 four-fold weft

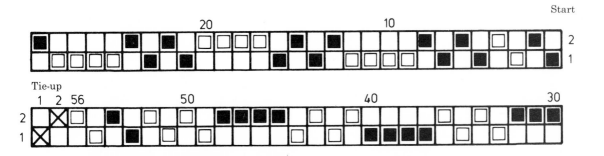

Start

Tie-up

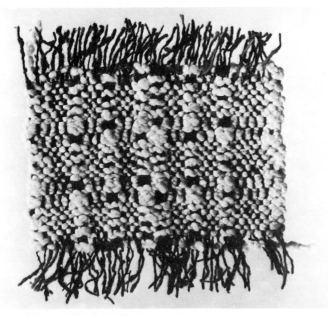

■ Dark
□ Light

To double or treble the ends,
thread two or three ends together
in the heddles

'Master Smith'   Detail of a panel measuring 0.50 m × 2.0 m, woven with paper and several different thicknesses of wool

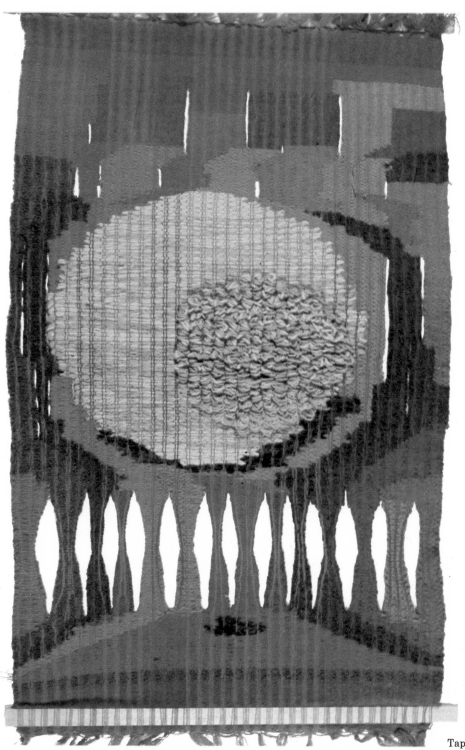

Tapestry with looped pile design

12   Colour and weave effect, basket weave

This basket weave sample is similar to the Prince of Wales check

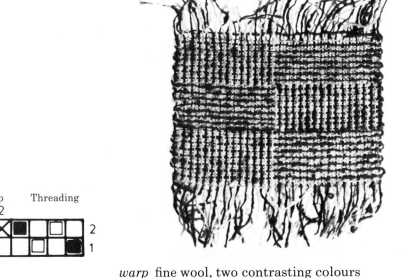

Tie-up   Threading

■ Dark
□ Light

warp fine wool, two contrasting colours
weft exactly as warp
reed 50/10 (12s)
threading single: thread dark light, 15 times; light dark, 15 times.
   Minimum of 60 threads for the effect to be seen
weaving 1 dark ⎫
   2 light ⎬ × 8
   1 light ⎫
   2 dark ⎬ × 8

   To weave squares, repeat each section × 15, not × 8. This threading can be modified by altering the lengths of the blocks.

13   Heavy texture in the weft. Pattern for a rug or mat
warp thread in two tones
weft heavy rug wool
reed 20/10 (5s)
threading two threads per heddle
reed number of ends per dent 2 or 4, empty dent, 0.
   2, 2, 0, 4, 2, 2, 0, 4, 0, 4, 0. Repeat this group for the width of the warp.
   Minimum of 30 threads for a repeat.
   The weft is too thick for a shuttle, so has to be wound onto a special rug shuttle

Rug shuttle

62

weaving $\left.\begin{matrix} 1 \\ 2 \end{matrix}\right\}$ × 3 single weft

1 single weft
2 double weft
$\left.\begin{matrix} 1 \\ 2 \end{matrix}\right\}$ × 2 single weft
1 single weft
2 double weft

Repeat from the beginning or use an irregular wefting. Heavy beat on an open shed.

■ Dark
△ Light

14 Tapestry with looped pile design. (See colour plate, p. 61).
The circles can be cut out of paper and pinned to the warp as patterns. Each row of loops is knotted round a stick to keep the loops all the same length.

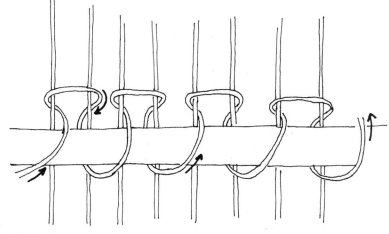

The stick is a length gauge for the pile and is withdrawn after each row

$\left.\begin{matrix} 1 \\ 2 \end{matrix}\right\}$ Plain weave

1 Pile row

$\left.\begin{matrix} 2 \\ 1 \end{matrix}\right\}$ Plain weave

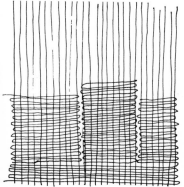

Vertical blocks woven without interlacing

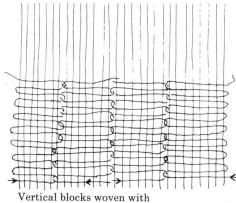

Vertical blocks woven with interlacing

Panel measuring 0.60 m × 1.0 m,
woven in small blocks with slots
left between them. This is the
Scandinavian 'kilim' technique

64

2 Three-shaft Weaving

A three-shaft harness is still rather limited in its possibilities, though it is better than a two-shaft harness.

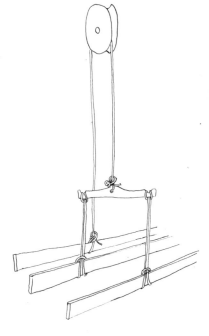

Mounting for a three-shaft harness

1 'Jean' twill
warp fine wool
weft wool bouclé
reed 30/10 (8s)
threading double in heddles and reed
weaving double thread throughout

weft-faced twill		*warp-faced twill*	
left hand	right hand	left hand	right hand
1	3	1 2	3 1
2	2	2 3	2 3
3	1	3 1	1 2
1	3	1 2	3 1
2	2	2 3	2 3
3	1	3 1	1 2

For a waved twill, work forwards and backwards, e.g. 1, 2, 3, 2, 1, 2, 3 . . .

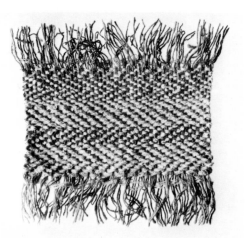

Tie-up   Threading

65

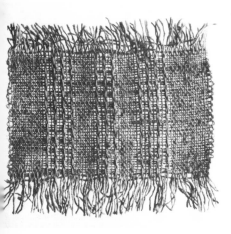

2 Swedish lace weave, with stripe effects running warp-way (Myggtjäll)

warp fine wool
weft rough-spun linen
reed 40/10 (10s)
threading single in the heddles
reed AB 1 end per dent
    BC miss one dent
    CD thread: 3, 0, 1, 0, and repeat
    Minimum of 32 threads for a repeat.
weaving 1, 2, 3, 2, 1, 2, 3, 2, . . . loose beat on a closed shed

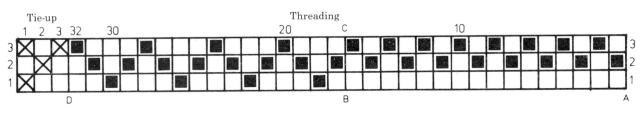

3 Variation of three-shaft twill

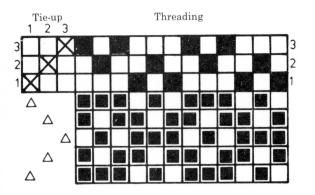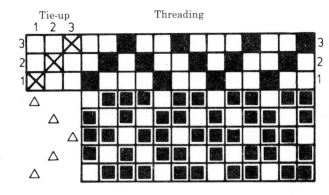

3 Four-shaft Weaving

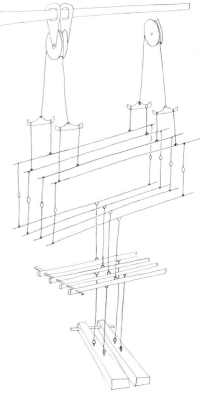

A four-shaft harness has fourteen possible combinations of lifting:

4 single shafts; 1, 2, 3, 4.
4 pairs of shafts; 1 2, 2 3, 3 4, 4 1.
4 sets of three shafts; 1 2 3, 2 3 4, 3 4 1, 4 1 2.
2 plain weave pairs; 1 3, 2 4.

Usually a four-shaft loom has 4 or 6 treadles. The simplest tie-up is one shaft to one treadle. For a weft-faced twill the order of treadling is 1, 2, 3, 4. For a balanced twill it is 1 2, 2 3, 3 4, 4 1. Plain weave is 1 3, 2 4.

When the loom has 6 treadles, the two outside treadles are tied up for plain weave.

Tie-up for plain weave on a
four-shaft counterbalanced loom

1 The arrangement of the treadles for twill

When a loom has only four treadles, the best arrangement is that given in the diagram, 1, 3, 4, 2.

Plain weave is woven using the left foot on both left-hand treadles 1 and 3 together and the right foot on both right-hand treadles 2 and 4 together.

A weft-faced twill is woven using the left and right feet alternately, left 1, right 2, left 3, right 4.

The quickest way of weaving a balanced twill is to place the toes on the outside treadles and the heels on the inside treadles. The treadling will be:

1 2, left toe, right toe
2 3, left heel, right toe
3 4, left heel, right heel
4 1, left toe, right heel

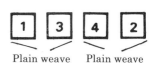

Plain weave   Plain weave

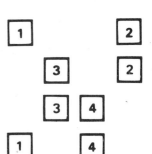

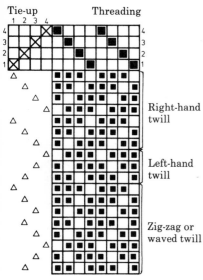

Tie-up   Threading

Right-hand twill

Left-hand twill

Zig-zag or waved twill

2 Twill weaves

Warp-faced left-hand twill

The diagonal line of the twill runs upwards to the left. The order of treadling is 1, 2, 3, 4. The weft thread goes over the first warp thread and under the next three, and this sequence of over one under three is moved one warp thread to the left on each successive row of weft, i.e. row 1 over 1 under 2 3 4; row 2 over 2 under 3 4 1; row 3 over 3 under 4 1 2; row 4 over 4 under 1 2 3. The fifth row is the same as the first, etc.

Warp-faced right-hand twill

Instead of treadling 1, 2, 3, 4, the order is reversed to 4, 3, 2, 1. This reverses the direction of the twill line in the cloth.

A zig-zag or waved twill results from alternating right- and left-hand twills. There is an almost endless variety of twill weaves.

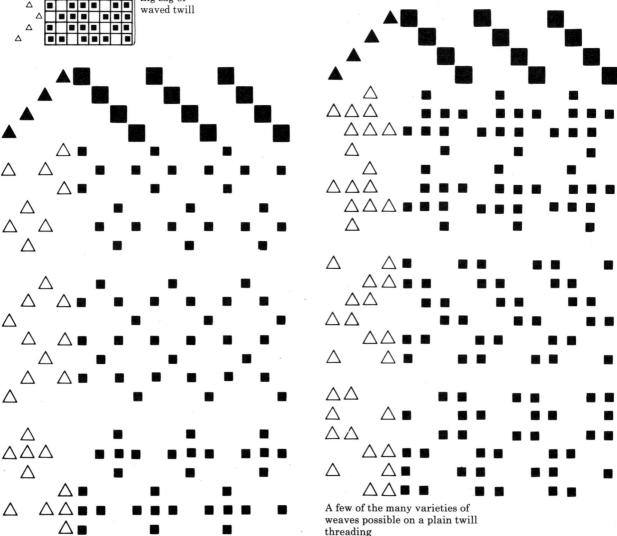

A few of the many varieties of weaves possible on a plain twill threading

3 Striped warp. Waved twill with a mixture of warp-faced and balanced twills

warp fine wool in two tones
weft cotton bouclé
reed 50/10 (12s)
threading single
weaving A right-hand twill, 1, 2, 3, 4.
        B left-hand twill 3, 2, 1, 4; then 4 3, 3 2, 2 1, 1 4, . . .
        C right-hand twill 1, 2, 3, 4
        D left-hand balanced twill followed by right-hand twill,
        1 2, 2 3, 3 4, 4 1, 3 4, 2 3, 1 2, . . .

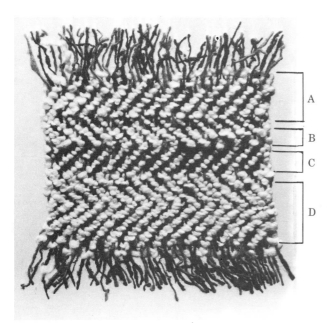

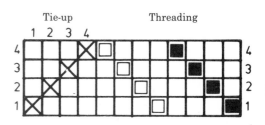

Right- and left-hand twill in raised
bands obtained by mixing
warp-faced and weft-faced twills

4 Diamond twill. Pattern for a rug

warp rough-spun unbleached wool
weft thick natural wool
reed 30/10 (8s)
threading single, 23 threads for one repeat
weaving 1, 2, 3, 4, × 3 ⎫
        3, 2, 1, 4, × 3 ⎬ repeat

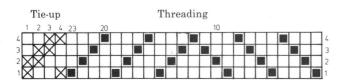

5 Twilled rib effect

warp thick cotton
weft the same yarn, doubled
reed 15/10 (4s)
threading double in heddles and reed
weaving 1, 2, 3, 4 . . .

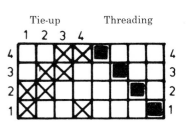

6 Rosepath, Swedish twill weave design (Rosengång)

(See colour plates, p. 72 & 73).
warp fine wool, two tones
weft a contrasting colour
reed 50/10 (12s)
threading single, 8 threads per repeat

weaving	1 or	3 or	2 or	1 or	1 or	3
	2	2	1	3	2	4
	3	1	4	4	3	1
	4	4	3	2	4	2
			4		1	3
			1		4	2
					3	1
					2	4

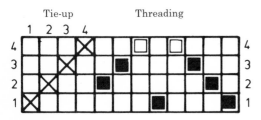

This traditional pattern has very rich possibilities. It is all woven in a plain twill, and can have a straight tie-up (one shaft to each treadle). The warp can be plain, or can have wide or narrow stripes.

■ Dark
□ Light

The general effect is often improved by separating each band of pattern from the next by a stripe of plain twill in the warp colour. If two treadles are tied-up for plain weave, a ground can be woven on alternate rows. This gives considerable scope for modifying the pattern. For example, tie shafts 1, 3 to treadle A; 2, 4 to treadle B

weave	1 or	4
	A	A
	1	3
	B	B
	2	2
	A	A
	2	1
	B	B

70

7 Variation of basket weave

warp fine wool in two contrasting tones
weft as warp
reed 50/10 (12s)
threading single AB × 4
BC × 4 ⎫
AB × 8 ⎬ repeat
BC × 8 ⎭

weaving 1 2 dark
2 4 light
2 3 dark
1 3 light
3 4 dark
2 4 light
4 1 dark
1 3 light   and repeat

The colour and weave effect depends on the precise order of light and dark threads, which must be contrasting in tone

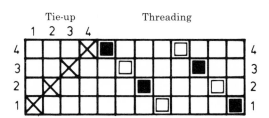

Tie-up   Threading

■ Dark
□ Light

8 Danish design, chain stripe

warp unbleached rough-spun wool
weft natural rough-spun wool
reed 30/10 (8s)
threading single
weaving 1 ⎫
2 ⎬ repeat
1 ⎬
3 ⎭

Treadle one is the pattern treadle, treadles two and three are plain weave.

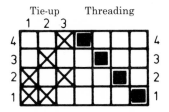

Tie-up   Threading

left
Rosepath
Simple tie-up, one shaft
per treadle. Woven with
two shuttles, one each for
the ground and the
pattern wefts

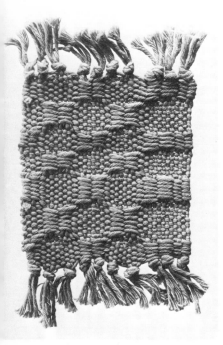

9 Swedish design, M's and O's, (Sålldräll)

warp cotton
weft as warp
reed 30/10 (8s)
threading single (at least 32 threads plus selvedges AB and FG for
a sample)
AB × 2
BC × 1, 2 or 3
CD × 1, 2 or 3
Blocks BC and CD can be different lengths
DE = BC, EF = CD, FG = AB

weaving $\left.\begin{matrix}1\\2\end{matrix}\right\} \times 6$ or $\left.\begin{matrix}1\\2\end{matrix}\right\} \times 2$

$\left.\begin{matrix}3\\4\end{matrix}\right\} \times 6$ $\left.\begin{matrix}3\\4\end{matrix}\right\} \times 2$

repeat repeat
large and small blocks can be alternated in the weaving

The stripes in the warp correspond
to blocks of threading

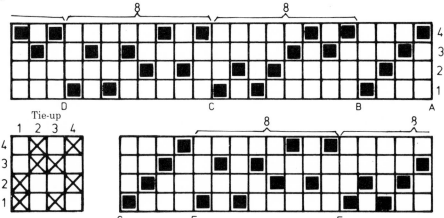

10 Little stars. Traditional French pattern

warp fine unbleached wool
weft dark natural wool
reed 80/10 (20s)
threading double in heddles and reed, 14 threads per repeat
weaving treadles 1, 2, for plain weave
    treadles 3, 4, for the pattern

$$\left.\begin{array}{c}1\\3\\2\\3\end{array}\right\}\text{repeat or}\quad\left.\begin{array}{c}1\\4\\2\\4\end{array}\right\}\text{repeat or}\quad\left.\begin{array}{c}1\\3\\2\\4\end{array}\right\}\text{repeat}$$

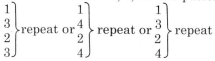

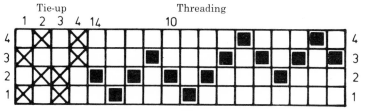

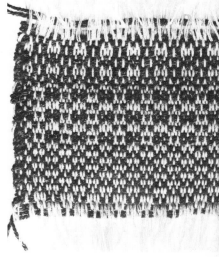

'Little Stars', traditional French design

11 Traditional Honeycomb pattern

warp cotton
weft as warp
reed 30/10 (8s)
threading single, 12 threads per repeat, AB is the selvedge
weaving start with plain weave (1 3, 2 4), for a few cm (ins.).
pattern 1&3, × 1 thick or doubled weft

$$\left.\begin{array}{c}2\\1\end{array}\right\}\times 3\text{ single weft}$$

2&4 × 1 thick or doubled weft

$$\left.\begin{array}{c}3\\4\end{array}\right\}\times 3\text{ single weft}$$

    repeat

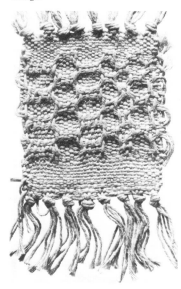

This draft can be interpreted in several different ways, with regular or irregular cells and with or without coloured divisions between the cells

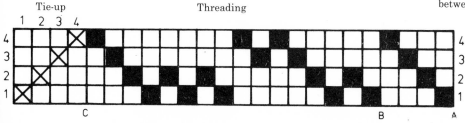

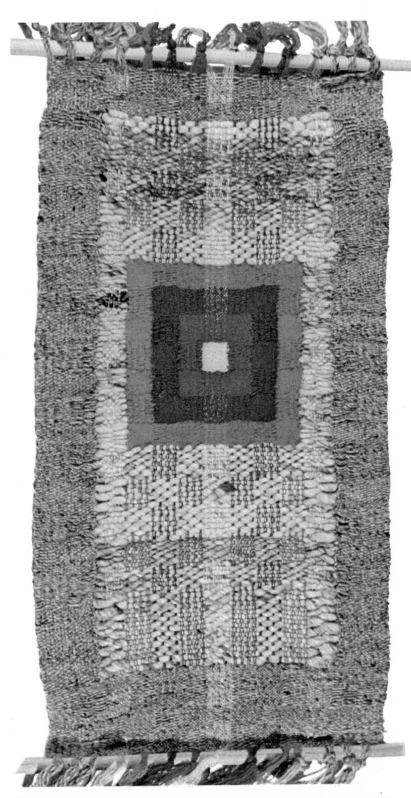

Variation of M's and O's, woven
with one shuttle

12   Spots in relief

warp rough-spun wool singles
weft as warp
reed 40/10 (10s)
threading single, 10 threads per repeat
weaving plain weave is on 1 and 2

       1
       2
       spot 1: 4, 1, 6, 2, 1, 6, 2, 4
       1
       2
       spot 2: 3, 1, 5, 2, 1, 5, 2, 3

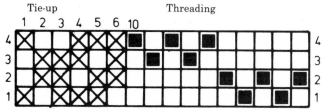

13 Traditional Danish pattern (canvas weave stripe)

warp fine wool

weft wool bouclé or linen

reed 80/10 (20s)

threading double in the heddles, 35 threads per repeat

reed AB is a plain weave stripe threaded 2 ends per dent.
The border can be threaded 4 ends per dent.
BC miss one dent.
CD: thread 3, 0, 1, 0, . . . The end on shafts 3, 2, 3, MUST go in the same dent, and the end on shaft 4 is the single end. The empty dents between the triple and the single ends help to group the threads into the stripes that the weave structure is making.

weaving lightly beaten on a closed shed

3
2
1
2 repeat

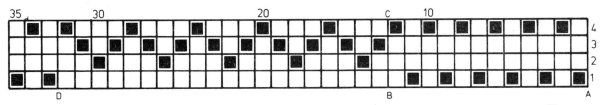

Tie-up

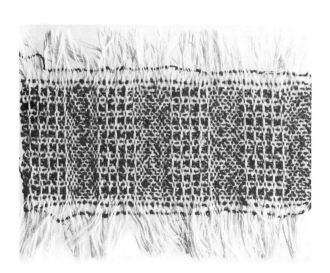

14 Pattern for a linen blind

warp natural linen
weft dyed linen
reed 80/10 (20s)
threading single in heddles, 6 ends per repeat
reed 3, 0, 3, 0

The group of three threads 1, 2, 1, and also the group 4, 3, 4, must each be passed through a single dent to assist the cloth structure in pulling these groups together. The empty dent between the groups also helps. The weft threads run in threes as well, and the weft grouping can be improved by beating the first two threads of a group very lightly away from the fell of the cloth and then bringing all three up together after the third pick.

weaving 4
        2
        4
       ——
        3
        1
        3

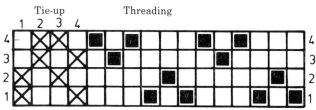

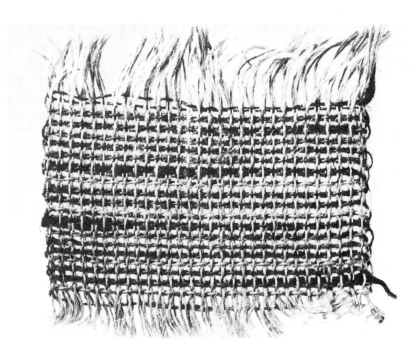

15   Four-block overshot weaving

Four block overshot weaving is a distinct technique, like damask or double-faced weaving. The great majority of the hundreds of examples which still survive in countries where weaving has had a long history, are woven on four-shaft looms. Two shuttles are used, one for a ground weft to weave the actual cloth and the other for a thicker, softer pattern weft to weave the design. The two wefts are used alternately.

1st row ground weft from right to left
2nd row pattern weft from right to left
3rd row ground weft from left to right
4th row pattern weft from left to right

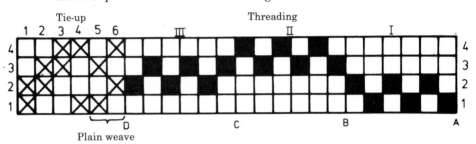

The warp is threaded in a series of groups on pairs of shafts, 1 2, 2 3, 3 4, 4 1, making blocks which are often arranged symmetrically. In the draft above blocks I and II are said to be 'on opposites', as one is on shafts 1 2, and the other on shafts 3 4.

If there is no threading draft given, the design is 'woven as drawn in', (i.e. as 'drawn in' or 'threaded through' the heddles), e.g. a threading 1, 2, 1, 2, 3, 2, 3, 2, 3, 4, 3, 4, would be woven 1 2, × 4, 2 3, × 4, 3 4, × 4

The most common designs are: rose, star, cross, diamond.

(i) The rose

36 threads for one repeat
threading AB can be repeated to enlarge the pattern
 BC the final block for symmetry

weaving $\left.\begin{array}{l} 2 \times 7 \\ 1 \times 7 \\ 2 \times 3 \\ 1 \times 7 \\ 2 \times 7 \end{array}\right\}$ for one complete repeat

Tie-up

Plain weave

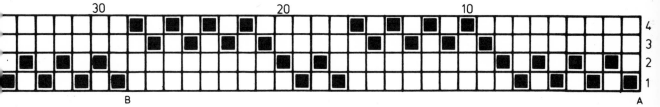

(ii) The star

This is the same threading as the rose, but it is woven the other way round.

weaving $\left.\begin{array}{l} 1 \times 7 \\ 2 \times 7 \\ 1 \times 3 \\ 2 \times 7 \\ 1 \times 7 \end{array}\right\}$ for one complete repeat

(iii) The cross

39 threads for one repeat
threading AB can be repeated to enlarge the pattern
BC the final block

weaving 1 × 5 ⎤
2 × 5
3 × 5
4 × 5 ⎬ for one complete repeat
3 × 5
2 × 5
1 × 5 ⎦

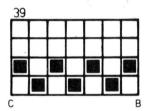

Tie-up

Plain weave

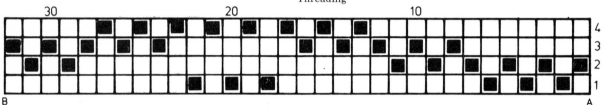

Threading

B · · · A

39

C · · · B

(iv) The diamond

This is the same threading as the cross, but it is woven the other way round.

weaving 4 × 5 ⎤
3 × 5
2 × 5
1 × 5 ⎬ for one complete repeat
2 × 5
3 × 5
4 × 5 ⎦

The Cross

The diamond

16 Traditional Swedish design, 'Monk's Belt'

warp fine wool
weft ground as warp
      pattern contrasting colour
reed 80/10 (20s)
threading single, 44 threads per repeat
weaving plain weave on 3 and 4

pattern	3 4, ×6	*other patterns*	1 2, ×8	3 4, ×8
	1 2, ×6		3 4, ×2 or 1 2, ×2	
	3 4, ×2		1 2, ×8	3 4, ×8
	1 2, ×6			
	3 4, ×6			

Threading

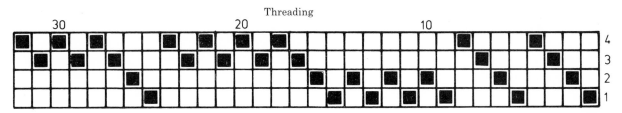

Tie-up

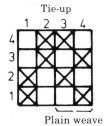

Plain weave

83

17 Crosses on opposites

48 threads for one repeat
threading AB = first unit of pattern
BC = second unit of pattern
weaving 1 2, × 8 (or less if very thick wool is used)
3 4, × 8
1 2, × 8
4 1, × 8
2 3, × 8
4 1, × 8

Threading

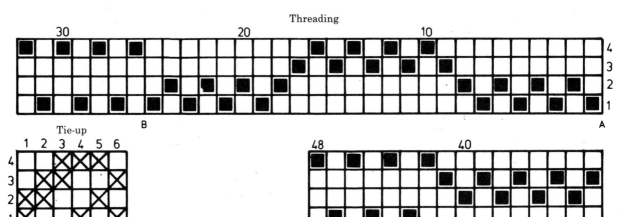

Tie-up

Plain weave

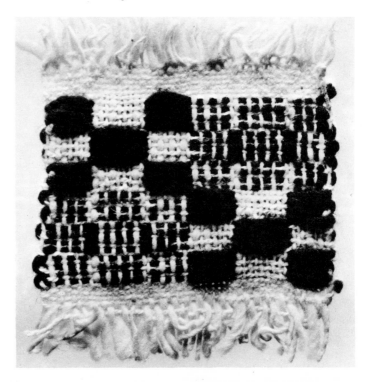

opposite: doors & windows. American Colonial.

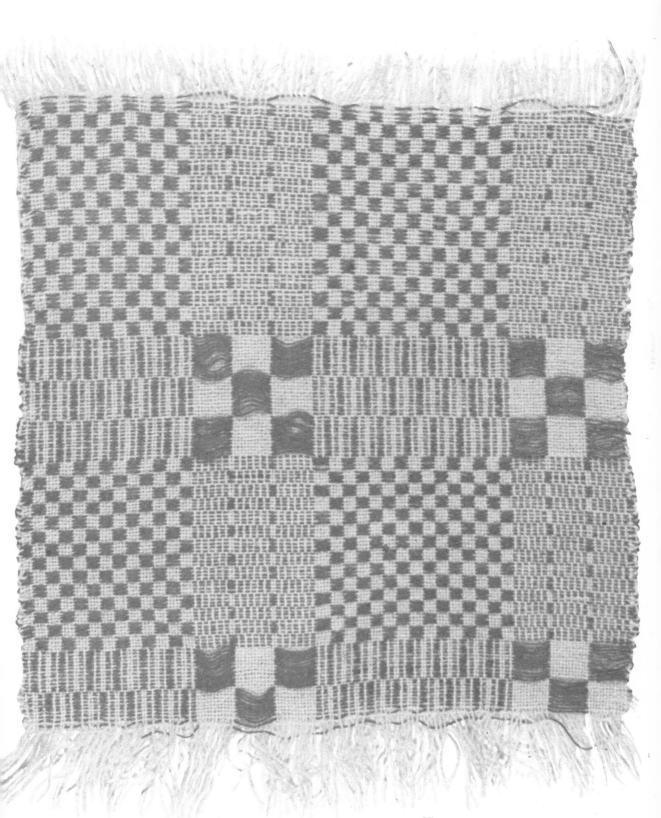

18 Double chariot wheels or Church windows (American Colonial)

warp fine wool
weft ground as warp
pattern in contrasting colour
reed 80/10 (20s)
threading single

> Table unit: (squares)
> AB, repeated to the length required, multiples of 12 threads
> BC, end of table
> Wheel unit (two wheels and join)
> CD, (wheel), DE, EF, (join), CD, (wheel), 105 threads

weaving 1 2, × 4 ⎫ repeat ⎫
2 3, × 8 ⎭ ⎪
1 2, × 4 end block of table ⎬ table
⎭

4 1, × 4 ⎫
3 4, × 10 ⎪
4 1, × 10 ⎪
1 2, × 4 ⎬ wheel
4 1, × 10 ⎪
3 4, × 10 ⎪
4 1, × 4 ⎭

1 2, × 4 ⎫
2 3, × 4 ⎬ join
1 2, × 4 ⎭

(The illustration shows 3 blocks in the threaded join, 5 blocks in the woven join)

Wheel unit woven: wheel, join, wheel. Follow by table unit

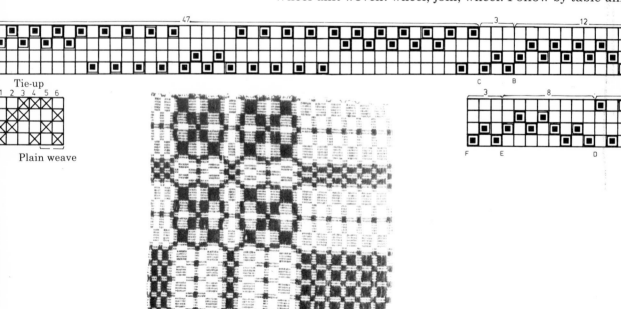

Tie-up
1 2 3 4 5 6

Plain weave

86

19 Doors and windows (American Colonial)

threading AB × 7 ⎱
  BC × 1 ⎰ repeat

  96 threads for one repeat

weaving 1 2, × 4 ⎱
  3 4, × 4 ⎰ × 7

  1 2, × 4

  (as above between 'wheel' and 'join')

  2 3, × 12
  4 1, × 12
  2 3, × 12

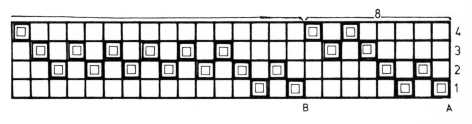

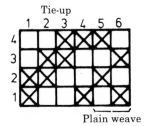

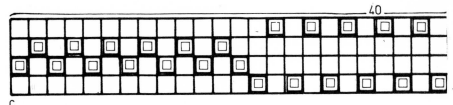

right
'Queen's Delight'. Design in three
tones: fuchsia for the ground,
(warp and weft), Pale rose and
vermillion red for the pattern

opposite
Double weave with one warp
green and the other white. Either
warp can be brought to the top as
required

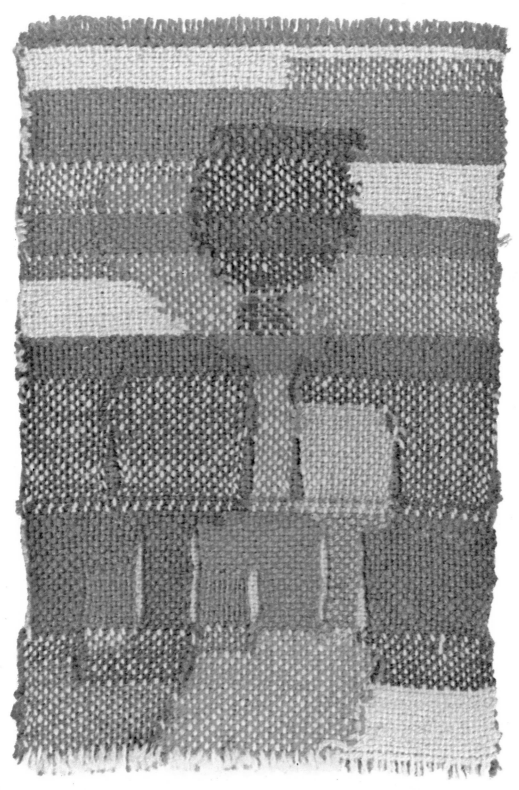

20 Queens delight (American Colonial)

threading AB
BC
CD × 8
DE
CD
DE
CD
214 threads for one repeat

weaving 1   1 2, × 6
$\left.\begin{array}{l}2\ 3, \times 4 \\ 1\ 2, \times 4\end{array}\right\} \times 8$

      2   4 1, × 6
          3 4, × 6
          4 1, × 1
          3 4, × 6
          4 1, × 6
          1 2, × 4
          2 3, × 4

      3   3 4, × 6
          4 1, × 6
          3 4, × 1
          4 1, × 6
          3 4, × 6
          1 2, × 4
          2 3, × 4

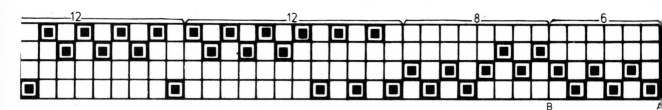

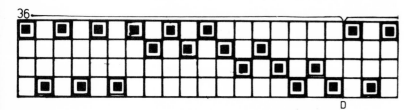

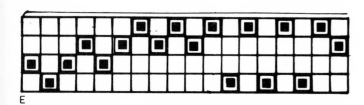

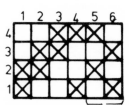

Plain weave

21 Double weaving

Two layers of cloth are woven one above the other at the same time. One cloth is on shafts 1 and 2, the other on 3 and 4. A double warp is made, the threading is single in the heddles and double in the reed.

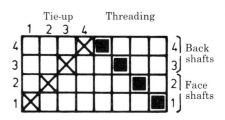

There are three ways of weaving double cloth:

The two layers joined at one edge only, one weft used.
This gives a double width cloth, as the two layers can be opened out after weaving.

row 1 2 3 4 sunk, 1 rises, weft right to left, top cloth
row 2 4 sunk, 1 2 3 rise, weft left to right, bottom cloth
row 3 3 sunk, 1 2 4 rise, weft right to left, bottom cloth
row 4 1 3 4 sunk, 2 rises, weft left to right, top cloth

The two layers joined at both edges, one weft used.
This makes a tubular cloth.

row 1 1 sunk, 2 3 4 rise, weft right to left, bottom cloth
row 2 1 2 3 sunk, 4 rises, weft left to right, top cloth
row 3 2 sunk, 1 3 4 rises, weft right to left, bottom cloth
row 4 1 2 4 sunk, 3 rises, weft left to right, top cloth

To make a closed tube, e.g. for a cushion cover, a few rows of plain weave on 1 3, 2 4, can be woven at either end.

The two layers separate, but crossed through each other to make the pattern. Two wefts
AB and BC are the units for squares dark on one cloth and light on the other. A square 8 threads wide would need 4 units of warp.

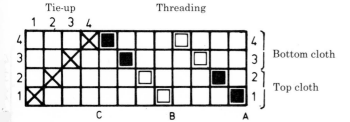

■ Dark colour
□ Light colour

row 1 2 3 4 sunk, 1 rises, weft dark, R to L, top cloth
row 2 3 sunk, 1 2 4 rise, weft light, R to L, bottom cloth
row 3 1 3 4 sunk, 2 rises, weft dark, L to R, top cloth
row 4 4 sunk, 1 2 3 rise, weft light, L to R, bottom cloth

The weft threads are crossed over at the selvedges to tie the edges together, when both the shuttles are at the same side.

The second draft gives a more even spacing of the warp. Shafts 1 3, carry one cloth, shafts 2 4, the other. The units are again AB, and BC. The weaving is very similar.

row 1 1 2 4 sunk, 3 rises, weft dark, top cloth
row 2 2 sunk, 1 3 4 rise, weft light, bottom cloth
row 3 2 3 4 sunk, 1 rises, weft dark, top cloth
row 4 4 sunk, 1 2 3 rise, weft light, bottom cloth

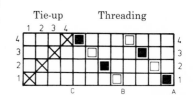

Examples of work

Belt

Rose-path threading
Threaded double in the heddles and
the reed, heavily beaten on an
open shed

Cushion

Waved twill with irregular
threading in the reed

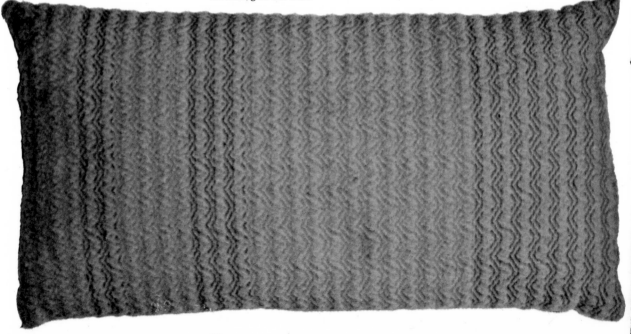

Bag

M's and O's threading
The strap is woven
like the belt
and sewn on

Irish necktie

2&2 twill, right-hand
The narrow part is woven without
the reed being used for beating.
The weft is pulled tightly to make
as narrow a band as possible, and
beating-up is done with the
fingers or a small comb

Glossary

Apron The cloth on the loom rollers onto which the warp is tied

Apron stick A stick in the hem of the apron. Apron rod (U.S.)

Batten or beater The swinging frame that carries the reed

Beam A roller or a bar across the loom

Beat, closed shed Beating after changing the treadles, for a weft-faced cloth

    open shed Beating before changing the treadles, for a firm, even cloth

Beater Batten, *q.v.*

Box, shuttle The box at the end of a fly-shuttle batten for throwing and catching the shuttle

Bout A group of warp threads warped together. Gating is tying small groups of warp threads (bights) to apron rod in front of loom (U.S.)

Breast beam The beam over which the cloth runs at the front of

93

the loom. Cloth beam (U.S.)

Cape The top side rail, or the whole side frame, of the loom

Castle A short, serrated wooden bar to hold the shafts while threading

Counter-balanced A harness in which the rising shafts are lifted indirectly by the sinking shafts

Counter-march A harness in which the sinking and rising shafts are both operated positively by the cords of the mounting. *See also* March, counter

Cross Interlacing of the warp threads to keep them in order. Lease (U.S.)

Cross, porrey The cross between the heddles and the back beam
    portée The cross between the small groups of threads used when warping

Cross sticks The thin sticks placed in the cross to hold it and prevent the warp from becoming tangled. Lease sticks or rods (U.S.)

Dent The space between two wires in the reed.

Draft Diagrammatic representation of threading or treadling, or the actual order of threading

Dressing Sizing, *q.v.*

End A warp thread

Eye Any small hole or loop through which a thread passes, especially the small loop in the centre of the heddle

Fell The edge of the cloth where the last pick has been beaten up

Float A short length of thread passing over two or more threads of the other set, in a woven cloth

Flying shuttle or fly-shuttle A shuttle thrown across the loom by pulling a cord

Frame, warping *see* warping frame

Harness A complete set of shafts of heddles. Harness frame (U.S.)

Heald Heddle, *q.v.*

Heddle The string or wire loop through which the warp ends are threaded and by which they are raised or lowered
    rigid A simple heddle of strips of wood, or wire, used for making the shed and for beating up

Heddle horses The short bars of wood from which the shafts hang in a counterbalanced harness

Hook, Reed Thin flat hook of bone, metal or plastic for threading a reed
    — threading Long thin hook for threading heddles

Jack Rocker, *q.v.* Upper lever, jack (U.S.)

Lacing Cords which fasten the back and front sticks to the warp and cloth rollers respectively. *See also* apron

Lamm March, *q.v.*

Leash A simple form of heddle

Mail A metal heddle-eye

March A transverse lever running across the loom between the treadles and the shafts. Any number of marches can be tied to one treadle and vice versa, according to the design being woven. Lamm (U.S.)

March, counter-, A march working in opposition to another. In a counter-march loom, the marches give the rising shed and the counter-marches give the sinking shed. Double tie-up loom (U.S.)

Mounting The whole of the mechanism for dividing the warp threads

Paddle A piece of wood with two rows of holes used for keeping the threads in order and for picking up the cross when warping

Pick A weft thread

Pirn Conical type of bobbin which does not rotate. Used in flying shuttles

Porrey The section of the warp between the heddles and the cross sticks

Portée A group of threads warped together

Quill The paper tube (originally a goose quill) on which a bobbin is wound

Race or shuttle race The heavy base of the batten, on which the shuttle runs

Raddle A very open reed with a movable cap, used for spreading the warp for winding on

Reed A number of vertical wires set at precisely defined intervals between two horizontal rods, used for spacing the warp and beating up the weft. (Originally made of reed, until the mid-eighteenth century)

Repeat A unit of pattern

Rocker The transverse lever, on the top of the loom, which lifts the shafts. Upper lever in independent-action looms (U.S.)

Roller The heavy wooden beam, usually round or octagonal, fastened in bearings at the front or the back of the loom, and on which are wound the woven cloth or the warp threads respectively

Satin Warp-faced weave without any definite diagonal line
    reverse Weft-faced satin

Selvedge The firm edge of the cloth, usually the last four or six warp threads

Sett The number of warp threads to the centimetre (inch)

Shaft A set of heddles on a pair of sticks

Shed The space between two layers of warp for the shuttle to go through

Shot Pick, *q.v.*

Shuttle Any device for carrying the weft across the loom through the shed

Sizing Applying a preparation to the warp to make it smoother and therefore easier to weave

Sley The part of the batten which carries the reed; the old name for reed. To sky is to enter the warp into the reed (U.S.)

Snitch knot The knot for adjusting cords between the various levers in the loom. Slip knot (U.S.)

Stick Any long, fairly light piece of wood in the harness
    back, front Sticks tied to the apron or the lacing, to which the warp is tied
    heddle Stick through the loops of the heddles
    shaft Heddle stick
    cross Stick through the cross when winding on or weaving, etc

Streamer cord Cord down the centre of the loom from the rockers to the marches

Tabby Plain weave

Take-up The contraction in the threads during weaving, caused by the two sets of threads bending round each other

Tenterhook A device for stretching the cloth out to its full width on the loom during weaving. Stretcher or Templet (U.S.)

Threading The process of entering the warp threads into the heddles

Threading draft Shows the order of entering the warp

Tie, long The cord from the countermarches to the treadles
    short The cord from the marches to the treadles

Tie-up The plan of tying the treadles to the marches etc., according to the weave to be used

Treadle The levers worked with the feet to open the shed for weaving

Treadling draft The diagram showing the order of operating the treadles

Twill A weave which gives diagonal lines in the cloth
    broken A type of twill which gives short diagonal lines in opposite directions

Unit Repeat, *q.v.*

Warp The strong threads running through the loom and lengthwise through the cloth

Warping mill A square or hexagonal vertical frame which rotates to take a long length of thread when warping

Warping frame A flat frame which is smaller than a mill, but takes a shorter warp. Warping board (U.S.)

Weave The order of interlacing of the two sets of threads

Weft The transverse threads in the cloth